Wyndham Ye

REGINALD BIRCH

MAGABALA BOOKS

EDITOR'S NOTE: Some of the terms used in this book, such as the words piccaninny and lubra, are no longer in current use, as they are considered derogatory by many Aboriginal people. However, they have been included to remain consistent with the vernacular of the time. Some names have been changed to protect people's privacy.

First published in 2003 by Magabala Books Aboriginal Corporation, Broome, Western Australia 6725

Magabala Books receives financial assistance from the Commonwealth Government through the Australia Council, its arts funding and advisory body, and the Aboriginal and Torres Strait Islander Commission. The State of Western Australia has made an investment in this project through ArtsWA in association with the Lotteries Commission.

Designed by Pigs Might Fly Productions
Typeset in 12/15 pt Berkeley by Post Pre-press Group, Brisbane
Printed by Hyde Park Press

National Library of Australia
Cataloguing-in-Publication data:

Birch, Reginald, 1940- .
Wyndham yella fella.

ISBN 1 875641 83 1

1. Birch, Reginald, 1940- . 2. Australia. Aboriginal and Torres Strait Islander Commission – Officials and employees – Biography. 3. Aborigines, Australian – Western Australia – Wyndham – Biography. 4. Wyndham (W.A.) – Anecdotes. I. Title.

994.1400499150092

This book is dedicated to Margaret who became my wife, the mother of our four children, and grandmother to their children.

'Time for a yarn and tea
We talk quietly, round the fire
Of our country, the Kimberley
Good memories, my mate and me.'

Acknowledgements

The author would like to thank the following people: Donald Birch, Ethel Birch, John Arthur, Donald Campbell, Donald Sharpe, George Pucci, Ngun Ho Lee (Bill Lee Tong), Graeme Ah Kim, Patricia Joan Mader (Mills), Margaret Menmuir, Ron Patching, Raymond MacNamara, Mona William, Jeff Clark, Dora Birch (Johnson), Ross MacDonald, George Edwards, Frank Chulung, Ruth Abdullah (Ogden), Dora Grant (Johnson), Hilton Gore, Roderick Woodland, Jack Trust, Daryl Macle.

The following people helped with typing and preparing the manuscript: Edith May Dryden, Roxanne Yamirr, Fred Chatelain, Jane Robbins, Josephine Marie MacNally, Joorook Ngarni Aboriginal Corporation. Special thanks to Jan Hutchinson for her editorial support.

Magabala Books would like to thank Brian Chapman for his invaluable support and assistance with this project.

Contents

About the Author

Reginald Birch was born on the Forrest River Mission Aboriginal Reserve in 1940. After being dumped at Wyndham at the beginning of World War II, he was educated at the Wyndham school, known as the pioneer school.

A musician, artist, peacemaker, activist, community developer, hunter, nature lover and humanist, Reg has delved into facets of life deemed impossible to most of those of his era. He became an avid sportsman, long distance runner, a rigger and coxswain on the Cambridge Gulf, an underwater and surface demolition diver, stock route worker, self-employed truck driver/contractor, licensed bird trapper, extended jib crane driver, forklift driver, fisherman, tourist guide entrepreneur and community worker.

His involvements in his community have seen him active in the local, state, Commonwealth and international political arenas since the 1960s. He has been at the forefront of Australia's major Aboriginal political developments and strategies for the past twenty-five years.

In 1990 he was named 'Aboriginal of the Year' in the area Western Australia North, which takes in the Western Desert, the

Pilbara and the Kimberley. The year 2000 saw him receive the honour of an 'Order of Australia' (OAM) in the Queen's Birthday Honours list.

Reg considers many of his achievements to be superfluous; they are only personal milestones. For him, the real issues are the outcomes of his community involvements and his activism, and whether people see and understand what's at stake, or choose not to.

When Reg was born the old Australian saying, 'fair go, mate' was widely used. In reality, however, it meant nothing for Aboriginal people or for much of the rest of Australia. These days Reg just gets on with his life, only asking for the rest of the country to be 'fair dinkum'.

Wyndham has been kind to Reg Birch and he wishes to return the favour. This is partly his story, and partly one as seen through his eyes of those immediately around him, as he grew from a small boy to an adult.

foreword

In the far north-east of the remote Kimberley, the Forrest River Mission stood stark and defiant amidst the beautiful wilderness. The river was idyllic. Tidal at this point on the vast valley floor, it entered the surrounding hills, a majestic cliff face on one side. On time, the rains had commenced. It was the wet season. The river flowed now with muddy water cascading down from countless tributaries on the mountainous plateau further inland. For thousands of years, Aboriginal people had fed their families from the land, sea, air and fresh water of this area. Even at this time in history, everyone on the Aboriginal reserve used the traditional methods to acquire food, no different to the previous forty thousand years.

This area had seen European visitors since 1884. In 1913, the first church officially began. My parents, members of the stolen generations, were brought in as children to the mission in 1922. The government policy of the time stipulated that children of mixed Indigenous and non-Indigenous heritage were to be gathered from the broad expanse of the Kimberley—and even further afield—and placed into institutions. Here, they'd receive an education in readiness for assimilation.

There was a vast difference in how each of my parents came to be in this exact location at the same time. They were each somewhere between six to nine years of age when brought to the mission. Both their mothers were Indigenous to this land called Australia and, unknown to both children, still lived in the Kimberley region of the vast continent, hundreds of miles away in a traditional environment.

My mother was abducted (stolen) by the Western Australian Police Department and delivered as per policy to the Forrest River Mission. My father was gathered up (perhaps stolen) with a group of about six other children from cattle stations in the Fitzroy Crossing area, taken to Derby on a wagon (dray), and left in the police compound for some considerable time awaiting a state ship. Here, the children enjoyed a brief respite. Worried, confused and homesick for their mothers, they ran away and began to follow the telegraph line, which they knew would eventually lead them to Fitzroy, near their homelands.

Unfortunately their plot was spoiled—they were tracked down, returned to Derby and placed on the ship *Bambra*, which steamed to Wyndham and then Forrest River Mission. My father never saw his mother again.

During its early settlement period, East Kimberley properties were mostly named after English places. They had names like Ivanhoe, Carlton, Bedford, Newry, Argyle, Dunham, and Lansdowne—the list goes on endlessly. Perhaps this was what attracted the destitute failures from the dregs of Great Britain to seek their fortunes here. For some, this Kimberley opportunity was the one specific reason to abandon everything and leave the place they once called home.

White women, however, were scarce and alcohol became the first companion of many in the absence of female affection, which had been so foolishly left behind. There was loneliness perhaps at first, the

yearnings for a companion. Then sometimes a boldness and sheer
recklessness told these men that they were their own masters. No one
stood in their way.

My father told me that he never knew or saw his father. Somewhere,
sometime in his life, someone had provided him with scant information
and told him his father had come from Scotland in the United Kingdom.
But that was all he knew.

Obviously attracted by the lure of instant wealth from the Kimberley
goldfields, my paternal grandfather had ventured north only to find the
visions of grandeur lost and shattered. He settled for a more sedate,
secure lifestyle and eventually became a mailman, delivering packages
and letters to pastoral properties strung along the course of the Fitzroy
River, from Derby in the West Kimberley to Fitzroy Crossing.
Somewhere along the line he met Dad's mother.

When Dad came as a boy to the Forrest River Aboriginal Mission, he
was called Sandy. He told me he was Bunuba by birth and was picked
up by the police at Quanbun Station. His mother was probably moving
among her people and away from her traditional Bunuba country,
further to the north. Other circumstances could have brought her there
at the time—perhaps she'd been taken there by her casual, white-
skinned man for his own convenience. Like most children from that
area with part Anglo-Saxon heritage, Dad had inherited fair hair, hence
his name. At some point, possibly through Aboriginal research alone,
his father was identified. The name Birch came to the fore but the
Aboriginal pronunciation finally settled on Burt. Thus he became
Sandy Burt, State Ward. Out of sight, out of mind.

As Dad grew, his intelligence developed and he adapted to what
were considered appropriate activities for a child on the mission.
Somewhere during this period he was renamed Cyprian Burt. Using

that name, he would marry my mother, Polly Ogden, in 1935. The original of their certificate of marriage is still in my possession.

Five years later I was born. When the war with Japan came to the shores of the Kimberley in 1942, we were evacuated to Wyndham, where bombs were already falling and parts of the town burning.

With all this going on, Dad thought it a good time to go to the Fitzroy Crossing area to trace his family and origins. He obviously found some of our kindred in the bush and on stations because they were able to inform him of his father's real name, Edward Birch.

By the time we left there and returned as far as Halls Creek, Dad was at last clear in his mind as to exactly who he was. I can still see him sitting, pondering on his life and all that had happened. He had been married just seven years and was already thirty-one years old. I believe that it was then that he changed his name to Cyprian Birch. Doing this must have been his way of uniting his Bunuba mother and Anglo-Saxon father. A way of future recognition and consolidation for all concerned—and, as his family, we have carried that name since, even though it is possibly still not recognised by Australian law.

Dad was always painfully aware of the troubles of the world. Many times my mother reprimanded him for bringing home destitute and needy people, both black and white. We had little to share but it was a way of life for him. And it's a way of life that gradually rubbed off on me.

My mother's father, a Norwegian, also had prospective interests that deteriorated as soon as his bank balance did. He, however, quickly moved onto cattle stations bordering the West Australian and Northern Territory lands of the Mirriwoong and Marlngin peoples, who moved freely across their spiritual country allocations, occasionally encountering European boundary riders, windmill repairers and general hands.

Early in the twentieth century it was common knowledge that Aboriginal people were beneficial to the pastoral industry. Slowly, many were enticed to live on stations and work for the pastoral owners. But by now, Aboriginal people were beginning to fear the white man. Some, a long way from their traditional areas, moved back onto the vast expanse of the Kimberley, but inevitably clashed with tribal people, the traditional Indigenous owners of the land.

Confrontation had its risks and eventually occupation wore down the existing culture. Our people were forced to live a life of submission and amalgamation. Aboriginal women especially became vulnerable, and many succumbed to the act repeated in countless places on this earth, the act that produced their children.

This was the case with Boonay, or Mary, as she was known on Mistake Creek Station where she finally settled. Like others, my maternal grandmother may have thought that liaisons and rendezvous with handsome white men brought rewards. She was a magnificent Indigenous woman, tall and dignified, and I remember quite clearly when I met her in 1952 for the first—and last—time.

Caught in the colonial web, my grandmother had two children sired by a white man. Since they were no longer pure-blood Aboriginals with obligations to the traditional culture of her tribe, the law of King George of England stepped in. Boonay's firstborn, her daughter Polly, was stolen by the mounted police and taken away. Her younger child, her son Ben, whilst merely a small boy, was quickly dispatched by her tribe further inland to stay with the Warlpiri people in the Northern Territory, far away from the clutches of the police.

Boonay mourned the loss of her little Polly. She did not know that her daughter was in the mission at Forrest River, a settlement near Wyndham. She did not know that Polly, as a grown woman, had married a one-legged preacher called Cyprian, and had three children,

Rosemary, Lawrence and Reginald. She would not know until many years later that her little Polly, daughter of the white man from a long time ago, was still alive and had never forgotten her mother.

The lives of my parents have had an enormous effect on me. It seems there's always been a hidden but devastating agenda that I could not possibly avoid. I was often a participant in, and witness to, not only many frightening and tearful events, but also many enlivening and loving ones.

In part, this book recounts the story of my parents' lives as seen through my eyes. It details their trials and tribulations as the 'new' history unfolded in and around the Kimberley coastal township of Wyndham during the first half of the twentieth century.

It is also the story of a small portion of my own earlier life and my recollections of people around me in the era from 1942 to 1954. These stories record the searing experiences in the lives of many people who called the Wyndham region their home, for varying periods of time, short or long, subject to their achievements, failures or demise. I vividly remember these stories and want to pass them on.

Wyndham was both bitter and sweet towards me in my youth. And although I realise that some of the content of this book may cause disquiet, I hope it will contribute towards the learning of future generations. These are stories that need to be told.

Reg Birch

Back to Wyndham

Back to Wyndham

From his vantage point on the side of the low stony ridge adjacent to the mission, the old man sat waiting. Deliberately, he had left his hunting spears back at his camping place some miles to the north-west. The word had already come; the missionaries had made it clear that no heathens could turn up and expect free clothing, to not work, and live there without giving up their cultural beliefs and 'pagan gods'. This meant that weapons and customs would have to be destroyed.

He had been there since sunrise and now watched the movement below. The bell in the valley clanged distantly and seemed to reverberate forever. In the adjacent billabongs, the brolgas seemed quite accustomed to the irritating sound and continued feeding and dancing. But the old man noticed some movement in the mission, where the mixed races lived, jumbled together and in obvious confinement, or so it seemed to him.

He had come in hopes of receiving food and precious other items that would enhance his hunting activities. Perhaps today, his relative who lived at the mission would make his appearance and bring him the usual things and maybe a pair of trousers to wear. If he did, he wondered if the others back at the camp would laugh at him and tease him for trying to look like a white man. Gazing down at his nakedness, he wondered why he was coveting the new ways. He was free as he was, with dignity among his kind. When he stood and spoke, everyone gave respect.

His thoughts returned to the settlement below. Unaware of the daily schedules of the mission, he wondered what was happening down there. It seemed none among the white people were ever leaving or going away for good; they were here to stay.

It was then he heard the sound, somewhat like the large bush bees, distant at first, then stronger, louder. He turned his eyes to the skies and quickly picked up the foreign objects, flying in formation and heading in the direction of Wyndham, towards the east and across the Cambridge Gulf. It meant little to him. He knew already that white man could fly in those things with wide wings. It simply told him that many people were going to Wyndham, but the reason was of no concern to him.

The year was 1942.

The Mission

My parents told us the story many times.

Early in the day, the small Anglican mission complex was already about its daily activities. Someone had rung the church bell and, as expected, the more devout among the newly converted Aboriginals began their silent meander through the conglomeration of mud and rock-wall huts roofed with thatched grass in the English country style. This was the test placed on the young Aboriginal married couples, now given the opportunity to exercise the new faith bestowed upon them.

Dressed in complete Anglican regalia the resident Minister, as if in defiance of any remaining spirits of the ancient Aboriginal land, stood tall in front of the church. Each couple, some burdened with young children, solemnly strolled past and into the new holy place. The Minister nodded, and gave a reverent smile.

'Good morning, Father,' they all chimed in response, knowing that once the rituals of the service were under way a period of about two hours would pass, then they would make a quick dash home, hastily grab their spears and hunting requirements, then off down to the Forrest River, a short walk towards the east.

The Japanese are Coming!

Down at the mission outpost, the early morning sightings had been disturbing. The missionaries knew of the Japanese invasion of south-east-Asian countries. The imperial forces of the Japanese army were continuing to amass, and it seemed further battles were inevitable.

A quick call by pedal wireless confirmed that the airstrip and fuel dumps in Wyndham had been strafed by Japanese Zero fighter planes. From a vantage point within the mission, a massive pall of black smoke rising from the direction of the town could be seen. Someone had burned the Wyndham jetty as well, and the previously bombed passenger ship *Koolama* had been cut loose from its moorings on the meatworks' jetty, eventually swinging away and capsizing, half submerged, with most of its cargo still within its holds.

At this news, complete turmoil broke out. Everyone was in a

panic. The church service was delayed, the old-fashioned organ played by the minister's wife droning away, helped along by two Aboriginal boys who pumped and supplied air to the worn reeds. The congregation would be forced to wait. Those inside the large steel-framed and corrugated iron covered building that served as the church had already begun to perspire. They waited in silent agitation, squirming in their damp, second-hand missionary supplied clothing. The sounds of the boisterous hymn 'Onward Christian Soldiers' spread through the luckless settlement.

There was a loud shout. 'The Japanese are coming!'

Exodus to Nowhere

When we could understand later, my mother told us that the missionaries had been instructed to tell the tribal people to go back to the bush and hide from the impending invasions. All the stolen generations children, now grown people with families of their own, would immediately be transported by boat to Wyndham and then trucked inland as far as they could go. The missionaries themselves would also have to abandon their station and leave for the south, or any destination they could reach as quickly as possible.

We were among the first to leave, and my memory of our arrival at Wyndham on the night-time tide is still vivid. Where the Wyndham jetty once stood, all that remained were the wooden karri piles still burning and looking like candles on a massive birthday cake.

The next day we boarded trucks, families all jumbled together, worried parents concerned about the unknown destinations, the lack of food, safety, no medicine for the sick. The adults were quiet. There was little conversation, our lives now so vulnerable, our future unknown. My mother anxiously questioned my father about what he thought they should do. Suddenly everything was so unstable; even the people in Wyndham were leaving.

There was really no question as to what must be done. Since the police advised everybody to leave, our family painfully moved into another phase of our lives. For our parents, it was their second time of being refugees in what was supposed to be their own country.

As we slowly journeyed inland, we found that the truck drivers knew of all the Afghan camps and deserted resting places from bygone days. Out of necessity, and with some foresight, these early travelers had planted vegetables, vines and fruit trees at various locations along the main roads and paths to the gold-fields at Halls Creek. Luckily for us, these now provided for our basic needs. We had no money, and everything we owned was carried in flour bags, blankets and billycans. But we survived.

Thinking it would be near to where his people would be, my father took us to Noonkanbah Station in the West Kimberley. We traveled with his relative May and her husband Frederick Gore and their two children, Harry and Rosalie.

On arrival, it was sad to learn the Aboriginal people of that area had also been told to clear out. There were few people to receive us. This was now wartime and our forced journey throughout the Kimberley had begun. Like our forefathers, it seemed as if we were destined to remain nomads forever.

Car Trouble

Somehow my father acquired a motor vehicle, purchasing this old, 1926 model, wooden-spoked-wheel Pontiac from goodness knows where in the Kimberley, most likely in Halls Creek in the south. I do not know how or when he learned to drive either, especially with just one good leg, the other a stiff, full-length wooden stump.

Anyway, once we had wheels, some form of security, my parents decided to leave then and there and go back to Wyndham.

Our search for somewhere secure to stay had already taken us over much of the region. But even after a short while, it became obvious that there were no jobs for my father with his disability. His work options were limited.

With a new wife and three very young children, Dad had serious decisions to make. There had been nothing at Halls Creek to provide for us as a family; we were different and could not slot ourselves into the local pastoral scene. And my parents did not want us to be only another burden on their relatives or schoolmates from the mission. They were all experiencing exactly the same difficulties as we were, even though it was their traditional lands.

An opportunity came with news of work on the old Rosewood Station. Partly too, we headed there in the hope of finding my grandmother and her people. No such luck. Her country was still further towards the east, near Mistake Creek and Limbunya Station in the Northern Territory.

Frightening Event

On this part of the journey we had a terrible experience.

Our old bomb was fully loaded and Dad was forcing the last bit of power out of it to climb this long winding dirt track up an extremely steep hill. The rock hole Jump-up on the old Lissadell Station road was notorious and had laid claim to the demise of scores of vehicles, all shapes and sizes. On the first run up the hill, our laughter turned to shrieks, as the engine died less than halfway up.

'Hang on!' Dad called out.

Mum grabbed us all and hung on tightly. The old bomb ran

backwards as Dad was unable to stop or lock anything. There were no handbrakes, virtually no wheel brakes. We clattered and banged all the way to the bottom of the hill. Billycans, swags, and bags flying off at every bump and jolting turn.

Luckily, no one was hurt badly. After a short spell Dad checked the old rattletrap of a vehicle. He unloaded all the gear we possessed and made another attempt at the hill. This time he was a little more successful. The road went upwards in a complete 'S' bend. He was able to complete the first turn before the engine again died.

Realising he could not stop it this time, he somehow jumped out. He stood watching. The vehicle rolled backwards. Thirty yards downhill it hit a big snappy-gum tree. Miraculously, the car held together. Only the back end stoved in, all four doors wide open, smoke and steam belching out, covering everything. Dad was overjoyed. At least he had conquered a small portion of the hill. That was a start.

After a complete check over, all the passenger doors wired into place, the extra heavy items off-loaded, he drove the old motorcar back to the top of the hill. We took ages to carry everything up the steep rise and then set up camp. The sun had gone and cold blackness set in to add to our misery. Only Mum could summon the energy to walk a good distance back down the hill to the waterhole. She headed off with two large billycans and an iron bucket, in complete darkness. I do not know how she ever completed that journey. Dad kept the welcome snappy-gum fire going but no one spoke until she returned a long time later. Our mother was the bravest woman on earth. She must have known there were ghosts, spirits, dingoes and snakes out there.

Rosewood Station

When we eventually arrived, Jack Kilfoyle, on the station, provided work and keep for our parents and we were grateful. However, this situation was difficult for Dad. As a roustabout, he was expected to maintain and build windmills. Rosewood boasted the largest windmill in the north, but with his wooden leg, Dad was not able to climb the structure. But my father never complained of his disability. He just got on with his life, and to this day I love him for that.

My sister Helen had been born at the station in 1942. Another mouth to feed. Now, with four children, my father's responsibilities increased dramatically. He had to find employment in keeping with his physical disability and the many skills that he had developed at the Forrest River Aboriginal Mission. It was time to move along.

By now, Rosemary, my eldest sister, was seven years of age. Laurie was coming onto five years, and I was a troublesome, mixed-up three-year-old. We all lovingly embraced our new baby sister Helen, giggling, cackling, and playing our childish pranks, not once aware of the frowns on the faces of our troubled parents, who did all they could to feed, clothe, and nurture us in spite of what must have been extremely difficult circumstances.

Finally, we left Rosewood Station to head back to Wyndham. We said goodbye to our parents' friends, Len and Ivy Mills. Like everyone else, their future was uncertain but Len was Caucasian and had quickly found work as a boundary rider, repairing fences on the outer property. They would return to Wyndham soon after and camp at the Nine Mile for a while. Then, Len was lucky and got a job at the Wyndham Meatworks.

In 1943 we began the journey back to Wyndham. News of the phases of the war in the Pacific had convinced my father that there were no better options and that we should return and take our chances. There were now refugees of mixed heritage all over the place and he believed we could do no worse than any other destitute family. In fact, although us kids did not know it at the time, we were worse off than most others.

More Trouble

We had all but completed our journey. Just twenty-four miles from Wyndham, at Goose Hill Creek, our old worn-out vehicle came to a grinding halt.

Dad's voice was urgent. 'Everybody! Get out of the motorcar. Quick! Hurry up. Go and sit down under that coolabah tree.'

Mum hurriedly dragged us all out, throwing us over the swags, flour, bags of clothes and billycans. Our bodies, still dust covered, rebelled. What was this new danger Dad was warning us of? Under the tree now, we looked back. Dad had already raised one side of the bonnet and was staring at the engine. We could see a cloud of smoke pouring out and hissing loudly into the air. He was afraid that the radiator would blow its top and we would be plastered with what was left of the boiling water.

'Be careful!' Mum called to him. 'We've had enough to deal with without another mishap.'

'It's all right. I'll let it cool off before I do anything. Blooming thing,' Dad cursed mildly.

But it wasn't only smoke we saw; it was steam as well. Everything had gone wrong.

So, here we were, broken-down again. Dad spoke quietly to Mum while she got the fire going. 'I think we'll be all right, just a split radiator hose. I'll bind it up tight with something, pour the last of the black pepper down the radiator. It might hold up till Wyndham. Only twenty-four miles. All that heat, don't know if there's any damage to the engine.'

He looked around for a while, listened to the screaming din of the cicadas in every coolabah tree along the crossing at Goose Hill Creek then strutted back to the old Pontiac. 'I'll get the last bit of salt beef out for dinner. We should be at the Nine Mile Camp this evening.'

No one responded. Mum took us for a swim before our mid-day meal. The water was yellow and muddy with clay but we did not care. The shady paperbark trees made it pleasant and cool.

'Plenty white people in Wyndham,' she called out. 'Hurry up and have a good bogey. Don't want them to see you dirty bush kids. Wash the snot off your face, Reggie!'

Mum sounded happy as she spoke. All her trust was placed in this tall, one-legged Aboriginal bloke who seemed to calm her doubts and constantly come up with answers to our unthinkable dilemmas. We children had no idea of the troubles we were in. A good feed, a ride in a motorcar, a warm blanket at night, what more would we need?

'Come on!' Dad called out much later. 'We're ready now.'

He had done his repairs, packed the old car; checked for compression with the crank handle and realised she would start up. 'Have your last drink of water from the creek now. Don't waste what we got here! Leave that full water canteen at the crossing. I'll pick it up after I roll start this old car.'

As he rattled off all those orders, only he understood the real situation. We all piled in on top of one another, laughing, grumbling, squirming for position, no cover, just glad to be on our way again. Mum removed the rock from behind the wheel, gave a gentle shove, and looked urgently at Dad. As the car began to roll, he waited for a while, then with his right foot, engaged the clutch. The old car jerked, coughed, spluttered into life and we were away. We shouted with joy, clapped our hands, and settled down for the dusty journey ahead.

After passing the remains of Charlie Flinders' store at Goose Hill, we clattered along the wheel tracks, looking directly into a burning mid-afternoon sun. Who cares? The crossing on the Kalamunda Swamp was rough as guts. I was certain the splintered old spokes on the wheel, already held together with Cobb & Co wire twitches, would shatter. But, somehow, it all held together. We passed the slight hill, through the old station on towards Wyndham.

Six miles or so down the track, steam and boiling water just blew over the top of the bonnet—and over us as well in the back. Dad must have expected this disaster because Mum had calico covers ready and saved us from likely burns. Dad, however, had no such protection and rode it out until we stopped.

Our screaming and shouting persisted for a while as we children tried to clamber out from under the covers, Mum arguing with Dad for not warning us sooner. Dad explained that he had known for some time what was happening and had only been trying to squeeze the last yard out of the old car.

'Shit!' he said quietly to himself. But the Anglican upbringing in him reigned supreme in this hour of reckoning. 'Blasphemy will not help the situation,' he reminded himself. 'Oh well,' he turned to us, 'that's it. I think the old girl's cracked an engine head. Got no choice, we'll just have to camp here on the road and see who comes along.'

Mum's and Dad's eyes met from different sides of the buggered-up old vehicle, both weighing up their individual responsibilities and concerns. Mum didn't say a word. 'What can go wrong?' she must have been thinking. 'Everything's all right. We're alive. And we've lived through worse than this.'

Waiting it Out

Two days had now passed. Nothing much had happened. Nobody came by, not even an aeroplane could be heard or seen. Just cicadas. Cicadas! Piercing, loud droning all day. And at night, the cold.

The dingoes circled our camp, frightening us kids. The young pups yelped and yowled, continually reminding their haggard-looking mothers of their ravenous hunger. Closer and closer, ever so close. Eyes glaring, dozens of them. We could not bear to look over our shoulders as we stared into the comforting firelight. Mum had no difficulty in controlling us. We could not understand Dad's calmness and lack of concern for the ever-present yellow dogs. He had more important issues to deal with.

Food was not a problem. Wallabies and kangaroos were everywhere on the banks of Parry's Creek which was two hundred metres away. There was a large waterhole, abundant with fish and water lilies on one deep section. It was towards the end of the cool weather and the pool was mostly shallow. The creatures of the wild queued up for their annual feast, as we the intruders created some havoc with their habitat. Dad also had acquired a .310 single shot rifle which helped a lot with our food supply.

Another day and night passed.

'I'll stay here and wait, just in case someone comes by,' Dad said quietly to Mum. 'You can go down the creek, get some water for the walk back along the road.'

This was no request but a necessary instruction to enable us to move into the next phase of our journey for survival. 'Give the kids a bogey*. Don't let them muck around too much. Today we'll have to walk back to Goose Hill Station. We'll give them a good feed of what's left for breakfast and then we're off.'

Dad's words came out slow and calculating. He had tossed and turned all night on the dusty swag. His mind was made up. There were very few options for destitute people. Hardly anyone knew we were on the road in the wilderness. No one knew we were isolated in the outback.

The sun had not yet risen. We happily chattered and played as we wandered down the lower waterholes of Parry's Creek. Everything was dry. The drab-looking shrubs were covered with powdered dust and brittle prickles and spines. There were deep animal foot pads everywhere, criss-crossing as they headed in the direction of the life-giving water.

Cockatoos screeched a joyous chorus as they fed, looking, as they moved across the ground, like an immaculate white carpet. They were reluctant to leave the creek as we drew near, disrupting their morning ritual. Splendid white gum trees stretched towards the perfect blue sky, now lightly streaked with high altitude cirrus clouds. Only the gnarled old paperbark trees dared to corrupt the scene, their huge trunks bent and distorted after countless years of flooding. Bark hung loosely, in obscene strips from the continuous ravaging of animals and our own Indigenous people.

Mum was pointing this out to us as we approached the edge of the waterhole when we all became aware of something else taking place. A weird sensation came over us as we witnessed for the first time an event that had been happening on a seasonal basis for millennia.

'Shh!' Mum spoke urgently. 'Here! Bunch up, quickly now!'

---

*Term commonly used for a swim or bath.

Danger! There was no need for a second command. The downstream end of the waterhole was alive with activity. A shallow layer of dust floated above the clay banks as scores of wallabies crawled over the leaf-covered creek bed for their early morning drink. As they approached, their instincts warned them of danger. Immediately, they scurried away in all directions, colliding, legs and tails frantically thrashing in the dusty, tight pads deeply worn into the banks. Some pads were up to three metres in depth, the result over the years of animals and erosion.

In their wake, the down river section of the waterhole was covered with a layer of blood-coloured flowers that had fallen off the freshwater mangroves. Soon, there were no ripples in the water. Gold and crimson coloured dragonflies hovered on twigs on the surface.

The dingoes found it difficult to trap the agile, younger animals who had already drunk from the waterhole and chose to wait for the slower, lumbering creatures that would sink into the quicksand always found in this treacherous creek bed at this time of the year.

The old man kangaroo had left his run too late. He crouched in the water up to his haunches, a perfect circle of clear water around him. His fur was completely wet. Small droplets seeped off his huge swinging testicles, making him appear grotesque and frightening. His continuous, angry hiss and huge, swaying body immediately struck fear in our minds. We could see his muscular chest pounding under the stained, tawny fur. This magnificent lord of the stony ridges was caught, isolated by cunning dingoes only a short distance away. His glazed turquoise eyes never left the patient predator lying on the sand close by. With an occasional desperate hiss, the old kangaroo waited for the inevitable.

Only one dingo had taken up the attack position. The others, with the pups, taunted the wallabies and waited. Even though just over a year old, the young male dog knew the drill instinctively. At intervals he would venture dangerously close to the massive, glistening black paws. If he was caught, he risked being shredded by teeth, paws, or the raking claws on the kangaroo's hind legs. Or he could suffer death by drowning. Although if this looked likely, there was always the possibility of rescue from the pack.

With the strengthening light, a new sound now pierced the bush. There was no wind but the air sang in a high-pitched breath and the tops of the tallest gum trees adjacent to the waterhole swayed and came alive.

'Mum, hey! You mob! Look!' Rosemary shouted, quickly alert to another sequence of events.

As our eyes squinted towards the treetops we could now see a flock of tiny birds, a mass of smoky green as they flew in and settled. Thousands of them. Instantly, their colouring changed as they delicately hopped onto small branches and turned to face the waterhole below. We marveled as we saw their glorious colours. Their heads were washed with glistening black and red, with pink and white flashes where new feathers budded. Their fat bulging breasts were vivid with violet, the border-line splashes in turquoise and a bright blue usually reserved for royalty. When they stretched and ruffled their feathers, it looked like they were wearing tiny, bright yellow pants. In fact, every colour of the rainbow could be seen in these tiny Kimberley creatures, the Gouldian finches. Among them, other finches soon appeared, again in various bright colours, all stunningly beautiful.

We stood in awe as the number of tiny birds increased, each one uttering its particular call as they gathered together. In swift, short, fleeting hops they descended the trees to the lowest branches. One moment the trees stood quiet and majestic; the next they were a mass of colour as small birds covered the branches. Then, with the sound of thousands of dry, high-pitched whistles, they appeared to melt. As one, they dropped to the ground, their thirsty chirping and the noise of all those tiny, fluttering wings blotting out all else.

'We used to see these sorts of birds at Forrest River Mission,' Mum said, 'but not this many!'

A good season had obviously provided the perfect breeding environment. There was a predominance of immature birds in the flock. Now, most of the little creatures were on the sand, moving towards the water's edge. They resembled a moving green carpet, splotched with every colour. It seemed every bird from the surrounding savannah near the foothills was there. Safety in numbers!

The arrival of the birds gave the old man kangaroo a moment of respite. He shifted his whole body weight off his haunches and leaned forward. As he bent to take a sip of water his glazed eyes remained on the dingoes, which by now were standing back from the edge of the waterhole.

We had dug soaks here, just days before. But the traffic of kangaroos and dogs at night and now thousands of tiny little bird feet meant they had virtually filled in. For yards around the water's edge the sand was smooth.

As we gazed, there came a piercing, stabbing, high-pitched call. Somewhere, unseen, was an ever-watchful sentinel among the highest branches. Immediately every bird made its getaway. Nothing flamboyant, just a low, panic-stricken scramble to the nearest bush.

The kestrel came in at an incredible speed, with the sun at its back. There was a sickening thud, an explosion of feathers, and a grey dove lost its life. Silence reigned for a short time. Several doves and finches squatted on the ground, terrified, too shocked to move. One by one they flew to safety. High in a nearby gum tree, the predator let the world know it was in full command. It had killed again. A mocking, guttural call came from its blood-soaked beak.

Almost instantly, the Gouldian finches took to the wing. Disturbed by the vacuum they left, dried leaves cascaded like fine rain down through boughs, while the occasional white feather from a bird's under regions glistened silver in the sunlight as it floated to the earth.

Within minutes we had forgotten about the dingoes. Mum, however, had not.

'Watch out now,' she warned, noisily clattering the large billy-can and steel bucket together as she walked towards the creek bed, shouting out aloud.

No drama. The wild dogs left immediately and we laughed at their hurried exits, bumping into each other as they squeezed through the tight pathway.

'Blooming animals,' Mum grumbled as we walked into the deserted scene. 'Got to dig another soak now and wait for it to clear. You can't bogey here. Water's too stink from those other dead kangaroos. Youse just got to have a wash out of the bucket.'

The old man kangaroo was still there, watching.

'Don't throw anything at him, you kids, he might come at us. But I don't think so. He looks near death to me.'

We all had a quick wash. It was easy, there was no soap. All the station-made bars of soap were used up, and the ration was small anyway. Kilfoyle, the manager of Rosewood Station, was a real tight wad.

Back to Goose Hill

Everything needed was bundled up with carrying straps. The day before Dad had managed to strip off the engine head with the basic but adequate tools he had acquired. He also cut out a few rubber strips from an old flat belt off a water pump and bore from

Rosewood Station. He would be carrying the four-cylinder engine head as well as our food supply, bedding, water, rifle, and tools. He could not afford to have his old wooden leg splinter and break off, so extra padding would not go astray.

We felt important as Mum gave us each a little pack of warm clothing, a small, treacle-tin billycan of water to carry and a snack of sugarbag honey which was found in special trees. She also carried a tomahawk and promised she would keep an eye out for more as we walked along.

Our spirits were high as we set off. We made jokes about each other and were amazed at the great number of flies that followed our smelly little bodies. Two miles down the road we stopped swishing them and they rode our backs all the way to Goose Hill Station.

All of us, except for Dad, were barefooted as we trudged along from shade to shade on the dirt track. My older brother Laurie would sometimes find a little energy and playfully strut along behind our father, mimicking his labouring gait as he stumbled along. My mother allowed this to happen, knowing full well it occupied our childish minds and took the stress away.

At the time, we never knew why Dad carried the engine part. Our thoughts were too caught up with everything around us. His plan was simple. At Goose Hill there were many old cars that had suffered the same fate as ours. All he had to do was compare the engine's cracked head with a similar one that was more intact than ours, strip it off and walk it back to our camp, miles towards Wyndham.

We would have a rest at regular intervals. Once Mum suggested taking shortcuts through the bush as the road wound its way at random, picking the harder ground and avoiding heavily timbered areas. Dad was adamant we should follow the wheel tracks.

'Someone might come along. A lost opportunity then,' he

retorted. 'Anyway, if I stumble and break my wooden leg, we may end up camping here for good.'

Mum never questioned his judgment. She was only thinking of us. We were growing weary. And now, sugarbag flies were also hampering our movements. Moisture-seeking and sensing the sweetness of the honey, they tried to cram themselves into the corners of our eyes, noses and mouths.

A Stroke of Luck

At last we arrived, tired, foot-sore, but happy. As Dad had predicted, the part he needed was there. In no time at all, he got to work and even retrieved other parts for our spoked-wheel veteran. His load would be far heavier on the return journey.

Meanwhile, down the creek, the catfish were biting. Mum and Rosemary piled the slippery fish on the bank, while Laurie and I busied ourselves flipping rocks and catching small black and brown frogs. Bait! Everywhere! Yuk! Baby sister Helen lay fast asleep under the paperbark trees, exhausted after the long walk, the hot sun beating on her delicate body which was covered only with a white flour bag.

That night we walked back to the ridge near the old home-stead and camped.

'Too many creepy crawlies down the creek,' Dad said. 'Some mosquitoes too. Need to be fresh for the walk back.'

He went on, comforting us. He told us stories. He talked about the places we had already been to, and about people we knew, reliving happier days. He even imagined out loud what Wyndham might be like after the bombing and burning.

'A lot of bomb holes around the Six and Seven Mile. Some didn't go off, they tell me.' The frown on his forehead got deeper.

'Hope that King River tribe don't go poking around for steel to make shovel spears and axes!'

He seemed uncertain about our future. I watched the flitting shadows on his face as the dingoes and curlews started their torturous howling and screaming again. Aware of my unease, Dad placed his powerful, oil-stained hand over my shoulder, comforting me. I loved my dad.

Blessed Sleep

The tapping on the side of the billycan woke me up. Mum and Dad were having a final cup of tea before retiring on either side of their exhausted brood. We slept cold that night, having only brought two blankets on our forced journey.

Dad reached out, stoked the fire, and placed the right sized logs on to burn through the night.

'I think this war's slowing down, in our part of the world anyway. Adolf blooming Hitler and his bunch of squareheads still going strong over there somewhere.'

He paused and waited for a comment. Nothing came. His information, we found out later, was months old, relayed on the pedal wireless through each cattle station. Aboriginal people were not part of this confidence and really had to squeeze such information from the Caucasian gentry.

'The Japs came close.' His mind shifted to another campaign nearer to us. 'But we'll be all right back in Wyndham. My younger brother, Donald, told me there's a big mob of Australian soldiers living there now, camped at the Twelve Mile. They've got a wireless station and the main camp is somewhere at the foot of the hills, he says.' A sip of tea, pursed lips, still too hot. 'Getting too cunning, he is!' He went on. 'The army's been wanting all the horses they can lay hands on and buying up all over.

'Don's got into the act, been buying a few, pinching a lot more. But they don't know, wouldn't have a clue. He's a bit of a clever sort, thinks nothing of cutting a fence in Lord Vestey's finest horse paddocks and bolting his choice across the border overnight. A bit of cunning works both ways, I suppose. The stations rip each other off. Poor old blackfellas get nothing. Don doesn't give stuff, as long as he's got his German Luger, salt and branding irons in his pack bags. Been getting into a few brawls lately, a bit chewed up the last time I saw him. Grog and womanising, I reckon. He's been skiting to me about chasing white women, too. He'd better keep an eye over his shoulder.'

The tea was now the right temperature. He noticed Mum was but a nodding acquaintance. 'Aargh well. That's it. Sleep.'

After a while, only a single cricket chirped away in the night. I gazed into the blackness of the star-studded sky for only a few fleeting seconds. I could not fathom the beauty of what extended before me; I tightly closed my eyes and snuggled close to my family for protection. I did not want to see the min min lights, the spirits that were obviously out there looking at me, waiting to take me on a journey, away, away. 'Don't look over the fire into the darkness,' my older sister and brother had warned me. 'Jarnbah might be there looking at you! That stinkin', ugly little bush man might take you away.'

I covered my head and blocked my ears. The spirits might even call my name, but I didn't want to hear them. Was there any-one awake to help me with my fears? Not even Mum! Finally, blessed sleep took over my wretched being.

Back to Parry's Creek

'Daylight!' Dad called out. 'Come on, let's go you mob.'

Even though the cooked catfish had been covered in gum leaves, wrapped in paperbark, and placed high in a tree, the ants still found them. No matter. Mum smoked them out, lit a bit of fire to warm them up, and we had breakfast.

This return journey was just as difficult as the earlier one. We saw large goannas that ran away as we came close. Mum wanted Dad to shoot one.

'I will if you carry it. My shoulder is pretty stiff and sore, you know.'

Away we went. The menu would have to change later.

About two miles from our broken-down vehicle, Dad sensed something. He looked ahead as we strode past a stand of healthy-looking bloodwoods and wattle trees scrub congested with rainbow lorikeets enjoying their late afternoon meal. His thoughts were confirmed. The evening sea breeze had come in across the Twelve Mile plains quickly. Fire!

'It's all right,' he said. 'Can't cross the creek, but we'll have a terrible night trying to sleep with the smoke and the thousands of wallabies coming off the plain, poor buggers.'

We had to be extra careful now, Dad warned us. Towards evening the smoke hung thickly in pockets of stranded air. Every creature—fur, feather, scale and otherwise—had now gone into survival mode and begun searching for safe places. As we approached our previous camp, we were surprised to see most things intact but the ground was smooth from the tracks of dingoes, crows, and fork-tail kites. We had thrown away salt beef, fat, damper crusts and catfish bones. The leather straps were a little chewed up where the wild dogs had bitten through them. And our old motorcar was completely covered in white bird droppings.

Mum walked down the road a little. When she came back she reported. 'No one's been here. No tracks. Only that big python, fresh track, this afternoon, gone down the creek.'

Dad noticed our frightened faces and tried to reassure us. 'He'll have a full gut. When he comes back, we'll hear him coming a hundred yards away. I'll just steer him around the camp and bugger him up for two weeks. The blooming soldiers, I think, lit this fire, probably out shooting wild turkeys. Got a load of grog and stray women.' Dad's face brightened up as he spoke. 'Sooner we get cracking the better. Tomorrow morning, some turkeys will still be there for us. Who said soldiers could shoot straight?'

Nine Mile Camp At Last

Somehow, my father untangled the mysteries of automobile mechanics. At last everything was ready and packed. Us children sat under a nearby tree, squished sugarbag flies and waited.

Under immense pressure from Dad, our grumbling mother reached over the engine, held the accelerator arm, and placed droplets of petrol down the open throat of the carburetor. This went on for some time, as Dad never tired of turning the crank handle. His hand was blistered, but he cushioned the pain with baby sister's sacrificed nappy and kept going.

Their efforts were rewarded. We shouted with glee, and jumped up and down. Our miseries were forgotten as once again we piled in. Away we went. Seven days and nights, an adventure we would never forget. Wyndham here we come!

The stones on the Parry's Creek crossing were rough but nothing could now stop our dust-covered chariot as we moved down the creek, onto the plains and the straight run into the Nine Mile. There was no grass on the plain; thousands of market cattle had put paid to that as they grazed slowly over the last three days of their journey.

The large billabong was now dried mud with scores of carcasses of skin and bone. Every clear walkway to the dry banks was marred with endless foot-deep tracks of the thousands of store cattle who had tried to quench their thirst in the thickening slurry that only months before had been a magnificent oasis.

'No use stopping here. There's no water, no wood, just flies, stinkin' dead bullocks, and the motorcar might not start again anyway.'

We drove on into the Nine Mile camp, straight off the dusty marsh country. There were tents and bush humpies everywhere. Civilisation. We had finally reached our destination.

War-Time Wyndham

I had never seen so many people in my life. The camp ground nine miles out of the bustling port of Wyndham was amass with the dregs of war, mostly Aboriginals, Afghans, and a few European local workers. Possibly a hundred people had vacated the township for the relative safety inland. The location offered water, shade trees and quick access to the hills and scrub should the Japanese fighter bombers of the Divine Wind squadrons come on their marauding excursions again.

My Uncle Edgar Birch later told us how quickly the Japanese had strafed the airport area during the attack on Wyndham at the outbreak of war. Taken completely by surprise, everyone had the living daylights frightened out of them. Uncle Edgar had been working on site at the time and to stay clear of the whining incendiary bullets, he depended on his long legs to carry him to safety. He said he thought he'd been doing quite well until some of the

26

Australian and American Airforce personnel overtook him in their eagerness to get to the tree line and hills.

Buildings, planes and fuel dumps were destroyed and a huge pall of black smoke covered the Wyndham area. The sighting of an extremely arrogant, cocky young Japanese fighter pilot flying low to observe his handiwork had rapidly spread the fear of the imminent invasion of the Kimberley by the subjects of the Land of the Rising Sun. Fortunately, no one was harmed and the only shot fired in defence was by the fiery old Scotsman, Norman Finlay, a storekeeper and gallon licensee at the old Wyndham town near the port. But Norman only had a shotgun!

On advice from the authorities, European and other citizens were directed south to Perth. Many local people, who could either not afford to leave or who chose not to, were camped at another location called Crocodile Hole on the Parry's Creek some twenty-five miles south-east of Wyndham. Those who had no choice, money, transport or friends dropped their bundle at the Nine Mile, where there was an abundance of branches, spinifex grass and giant boab trees to construct somewhere to live.

Food came on a regular basis from army supplies and was supplemented by bush tucker. Anything vital that was not issued to us was foraged from the local black market or simply stolen from shops in town. The Chinese and European storekeepers had boarded up their buildings for security and, having been reassured by the police, departed for safer areas south.

One night, one of our uncles snuck into some of Wyndham's unattended shops to acquire items like oil of citronella, Bex and Aspro powders, Vicks ointment, carbide for the lamps and wax matches. The shops were being abused on a regular basis so entry was not a problem for him. Once inside, he began searching in the darkness. He was interrupted suddenly by another intruder who walked boldly in and flashed his torch around. Alarm bells rang when Uncle recognised the local policeman who obviously had seen his sly entrance. He quickly hid, and braced himself for the inevitable. (My uncle was built like a wild bull and was known for his physical exploits.) Minutes crept by, the tension mounted, then came the realisation. The policeman was also a thief! Arms laden with contraband, he left the shop. My wide-eyed uncle then continued to help himself. The war had created a desperate situation for everyone.

By 1943, the outcome of the Pacific invasion was still in the balance. Battles were being fought close by on islands to the north. There was no radio so whenever army or airforce personnel ventured away from their base camps, they passed on news of the raging war along with Australian government propaganda and information on protection methods for the continent's defenceless northern shoreline. Nobody in Wyndham believed them, as we were closer to the battlefront than Canberra where the news for the general Australian public was being manipulated.

Our own Aboriginal men were able to acquire vast amounts of ammunitions, including valuable army-issue rifles and side arms. There was no telling when another land-based invasion would occur. There were stories of coastal clashes between Aboriginals and Japanese north of Kununurra and Wyndham. We listened wide-eyed to the stories of alleged killings, and remembered how, before the war started, bush people told of long black boats and unusual sounds at night in secluded deep-water bays north-west of Wyndham. Obviously, these were submarines engaged in surveillance for strategic future developments.

The Japanese presence on the northern coastline was not a secret. The eyes and ears of the so-called 'primitive' dwellers on the relatively unknown coast followed their every movement. In fact, had Aboriginal people been able to somehow record unofficial landings of aliens on our northern shores, it would have been common knowledge that we'd been visited for thousands of years.

The massed camp at the Nine Mile became home for a lot of us. We were the ones of no fixed address, of no consequence, and of no concern. Our parents merely accepted their lot and awaited the outcome of war. There was nowhere else to go. We had no money, no options, no nothing; we were only a band of people slowly coming together but not through our own choosing. But this was our home in those days and, as it turns out, in a lifetime we have hardly moved from this location at all. There was no desire to leave then, and none now.

Soldiers

As long as it was still wartime, all manner of mankind camped out of town, still afraid of Japanese bombing raids. We learned that people were camped out as far as Crocodile Hole, down on the Halls Creek road. Wyndham itself resembled an army base of sorts. There were four-wheel drive tracks leading off in all directions around the range of hills. The army had moved in and their responsibility was to protect this frontier township from any further attack from the armed Imperial Japanese strike force. Blitz trucks and utilities painted in camouflage colours moved around constantly, loaded both with soldiers in uniform and at times others just bludging a ride.

The soldiers were an amiable bunch and strove to do their job well. Dad had another opinion. 'They're just happy because they're here, poor buggers. Not too far away, up in the jungles on the Kokoda Trail and on the islands north of New Guinea, it's crawling with Japs. Blokes are dying like flies in treacle. They always wonder when it's their turn to head up and have to face up to live bullets. I have seen soldiers cry when they get drunk. They won't tell you, but it's all over their faces, poor buggers. Give up anything, they will,' he went on. 'If they can get their hands on it. Decent blokes they are.'

We soon found out what he was talking about. Simply to stop supplies and stores from being stolen, there were army caches hidden all over the foothills near the airport and the Six Mile Pub. But Aboriginal people knew all the hidden locations anyway and discreetly helped themselves at every opportunity.

When the army twigged to this, the local Aboriginal men were watched by police and soldiers alike. In the hottest time of the day, however, all off-duty personnel would be in the pubs. The rest, supposedly on armed guard duty, would be most likely be lying in the shade in some convenient location. With the temperature looming well above forty degrees centigrade, these recently arrived, pink-faced, volunteer, soldiers of fortune knew Tojo was not going to gatecrash their afternoon siesta, so why worry. If the Sergeant Major wants to fret about some poor black-fellas pinching tin dog and biscuits then that's his concern. Many soldiers wondered why the Japs wanted this God-awful country in the first place.

My father had friends who knew the routine for the army patrol times. He readily got information, possibly over a bottle of rum and a promise of more. Soon, it was not the men who carried out raids to acquire food and supplies; it was the women, our mothers who set out mid-afternoon to unguarded fuel dumps and food supply caches deep in the scrub. Us kids invariably went with them. Most of our excursions were disguised as goanna hunts or wild fruit and yam collecting. If patrols came by, they never questioned anyone. Just one glance would tell their status. Mum or my new aunties would say, 'They coming close to see if there's any single ones amongst our mob. They got their girlfriend already. Greedy buggers, they only looking for more. Must be got two pricks like old man goanna.'

On one such raid to a fuel dump, I suffered greatly. All small children were left behind. In order to make the 'collecting' appear authentic, only children who could walk were brought along. Extreme midday heat, mirages bouncing off everything, was the perfect timing for foraging. Under the camouflage cover, my mother moved swiftly.

'Don't go away, stay right here. Not long, then we're gone,' Mum said to me.

Too late, she realised she had not brought the tool to peel back the seal on the bung on a twelve-gallon drum of engine oil. Quickly she angled the drum so as to strike a neat incision with her tomahawk. With the first blow, the axe head buried itself. Her immediate reaction was to withdraw it. In her haste, the drum tipped over. Hot oil burst over my body. I screamed aloud in pain. Instantly my mother called to our Aunty Sue. 'You get the oil, I'll run back with this kid and wash him. Them blooming soldiers might hear him.'

Somehow, they still acquired the oil we needed to keep our old vehicles moving. I think the soldiers knew anyway, but nobody cared. I was kept in the camps for quite some time until the damage to my skin healed. No prying eyes at the Six Mile would be able to put blame on our family for the things we had to do to survive.

The Gully

Eventually, the war over, in 1946 we moved into the existing township at Wyndham Port. We lived in luxury in the Gully. My parents had bought this old, two-room house (for eighty pounds) from an old bloke called Horace Benson. He was ancient! Much taller than my father, with harsh red features, huge bony hands, he had a story similar to thousands of would-be prospectors who had made the journey to the goldfields only to return to the more sedate lifestyle of Wyndham and rekindle the trade he had abandoned in search of the ultimate dream.

Our new house stank of leather, curing spirits, and boot polish. Old Horace was a cobbler, and had obviously grown tired of his existence. The tools of his trade and dozens of boots still not yet repaired lay stacked on shelves, on the floor, everywhere, like leathery creatures with tiny eyes and floppy mouths.

We could not have wished for anything better. None of us children had ever worn shoes but now we clopped around everywhere with boots two or three sizes too large. There was one painful problem though. Horace had lived alone and did not care where he left his off-cuts. Tacks, nails and steel shavings off the old army-type Blucher boots which were popular at the time were all over the place. We regularly picked them up with our bare feet—inside and outside of the house—for years to come.

And we slept on beds. Wow! Everyone had a mattress made of coconut husk covered with light calico. Absolute bliss! These were easy to come by as the meatworks was well established and at its height of production. The West Australian Government employed hundreds of men and women and had many bunkhouses. As you can imagine, the lowly mattress had multiple purposes. There were no privately owned four-wheel drive vehicles, except for one dilapidated Ford Marmion Herrington. Everyone who traveled the dirt tracks of the Kimberley did so with an ample supply of mattresses, conveniently borrowed from the bunkhouses, to assist them in the numerous wet and dry bogs they encountered. We came along and just picked up the discarded ones. Thank you very much!

I quickly became accustomed to this new lifestyle, with all its new commodities and surprises. Best of all, Dad had a new job. Every morning before the sun had risen Mum would already be awake. From bed, we would hear her bustling around in the old kitchen, scraping the ashes from out of the huge wood stove. She used a heavy but effective tool fashioned by my father in his portable blacksmith's forge. (It was my job to wind the handle and keep the air supply going while feeding the coke and coal as he fashioned all sorts of useful metal objects on his huge anvil. I marveled at his handiwork and his quick ability to create domestic items.)

A few black pots and kettles of various sizes hung around the soot-covered walls, below the battered chimney. Mum was always careful to place the ash into an old iron bucket and not have it spill on the floor, as everything was difficult enough without making more work. She'd get the fire going in no time at all and immediately place the big, dented saucepan without the handle over the centre position on the stove. This contained our usual breakfast of ground oatmeal, which, year in, year out, went with anything else that was available. Two large soot-stained kettles of water would go on either side; one for tea, the other to provide warm water to wash off the offending body odours that always seemed to be present. They never bothered us but Mum had other plans, as usual. Almost as if on command, the water above the oatmeal mass started to boil and Mum would start stirring the thick porridge as it popped and bubbled like a miniature volcanic mud spring.

When it was the cold weather time, as soon as the fire was aglow, with a voice radiant with warmth, our diligent mother would patiently arouse and shepherd each one of us out of our sleeping places. Five ragged, sleep-infected children would then jostle and thrash out our pecking order in front of this blessed old stove. Shabbily dressed in clothes that served for both for day and night attire, we huddled together for warmth. There was one exception. Older sister Rosemary was a big girl now. Mum doted upon her and somehow, out of nowhere, acquired for her clothing befitting the European children from across the One Mile Gully.

Eagerly, we would listen to the bubbling porridge. Everyone had a tin plate which sufficed for every meal served. When it was done, Mum would announce 'Righto,' as she placed dollops on our plates, each adjusted to her estimation of our bodies' needs. Hungrily, we sat around the handmade wooden table. No milk! But in its place came a spoonful of dripping or rendered fat and cold damper leftovers from the night before.

There was no point asking for more unless one of us was ill and unable to eat. Leftovers were shared, or else you volunteered to wash up and scraped the pot of its dry oatmeal crust. Mum baked once a day—damper for us, and bread, which she sold around town to prominent European bachelors or families whose mothers and wives knew nothing about how to prepare this luxury but could afford to pay.

Almost all of these rituals at home in the Gully were conducted in silence. Unless somebody broke a rule or upset the next one. If one of us accidentally or on purpose farted, spontaneous, uninterrupted laughter would erupt, with finger pointing accusations until the offending odour subsided.

Such was our innocent, happy life then. Dad and Mum, I came to notice during this period in our lives, having not known anything else, reflected the values of the missionaries at Forrest River. Devotion, cleanliness, an outward expression of Godliness, all were part and parcel of everyday life. I understood none of it at the time. It was an extreme effort for me to keep clean, with snot always dripping from my huge nose.

Rarely was it cold in Wyndham, but when the cold snaps did occur, we got severe chilblains on our cheeks, wrists, fingers, and ankles. Our brown skins cracked and bled. It was nothing new to any of us, just something we confronted year in, year out.

Mum and Dad quoted the Saint James Bible on a daily basis. One result of their devout Anglican upbringing was that they were obliged to pass on their newfound wisdom. They told us there was a God, a spiritual being which controlled our destiny. It seemed to me that everything we dearly loved and physically enjoyed was called sin. Exclamations such as 'Oh shit!' were not tolerated and we suffered the consequences for our mis-demeanors. Not to be outdone, we quickly switched to the Aboriginal language our parents had inherited from the Forrest River Mission tribal people and used the dialect to express our frustrations.

Kimberley Men

Dad would talk at times to his brothers Edgar and Donald, and his mates, Alec Menmuir, Richard Macale, Jack Brumbie, Gerald Beatie and Ernie Chapman. Some of these men had grown up with him at Forrest River Mission; the rest were Aboriginal relatives and workers from surrounding cattle stations. They would talk of post-war development and what was happening to the Kimberley; they spoke of the pastoral industry, and what was thought of as the growing Aboriginal problem.

These men were well placed in the East Kimberley industry. Every opportunity was taken to share their feelings and progress as they moved—or rather pressured their way—into the emerging social structure. They were Aboriginal, or were they really? The full-blooded Indigenous person treated them with mistrust, and so they should. It was not their country, their skin was brown, they spoke the English language, and were perceived in very much the same way as the whitefellas. For the tribal Aboriginals, the threat of danger and domination was always present.

Our parents were being hounded as part of that bitter process of assimilation. They would become the first generation living without the Dreaming. Our Dreaming! The Dreaming that should have been there for us but which was now denied by both sides, the white and black. It was no fault of our parents and their own kind. Somehow they had to survive this assimilation. The only hope was to communicate with each other and draw on the remains of the fragmented spirituality they inherited from their black mothers. There was no help coming from the other side—only the growing call for more native reserves, native hospitals, native compounds, native welfare. In other words, it was segregation. As Aboriginals, we had no future.

Dad's brothers and close friends became extremely defiant. They were ready to defend their small patches of property from which they derived a livelihood. Quickly they adopted the language of the particular Aboriginal group they moved among. At the same time they polished their etiquette in order to deal with the lumbering giant, the Union Jack. Unfortunately, they were not always successful. As a boy I witnessed many brutal stoushes, much blood and misery, and all in the name of the colour of your skin.

Both my father's brothers were flamboyant characters, hard riders and fighters with a bite in their tongue and warrant stories of their own. Richard Macale, however, was completely different. Also a refugee from Forrest River Mission, his first skill was stock work, as expected. Then, as the situation changed, he did anything and everything. He had been a guide for naval operations during World War II along the Cambridge Gulf and north-east Kimberley coastline. The skills he acquired then provided him with the opportunity to build his own boat from bush timber acquired on the Aboriginal reserve.

He gave his boat the name *Mulanjuna* from the place where he cut the timber. About twenty feet long and boasting sails and an inboard motor, it was used for transport by the locals, the mission, and the police department (for search and rescue). It also provided me, when I was about twelve years old, with my first real experience of the sea.

Richard Macale had left the mission early in the war years and found work on a station, which is now Diggers Rest. Later, he bought a truck and was employed on the construction of Ivanhoe Crossing bridge (near Kununurra). Quick to adapt to change, he drove mobile cranes and blocked winches used in jetty constructions. It was Richard who taught me to skull, using just one oar to manipulate wooden clinker boats on the Cambridge Gulf's treacherous tidal waters.

Jack Brumbie was my mother's relative from the Northern Territory. A war veteran who had experienced horrific campaigns in the islands to the north of Australia, he was a recipient of a medal for extreme bravery. He was shattered when he came to Wyndham. As a soldier, his contribution was the same as anyone's, and while he was serving he was respected for it. But here, back in Australia, he was not. He was not even a citizen of the country he fought for! Such was his lowness of feeling, he was continually being thrown into gaol for drinking. A tough stockman and yard builder, he had stood up and defended what he thought was his right. Finally, completely disillusioned, he wandered away, to an unknown destination forever.

Gerald Beatie was a huge man, the first bald-headed Aboriginal I ever saw. He hardly ever spoke but when he laughed he emitted a throaty whistle. His specialty was windmill and tank construction on surrounding cattle stations. Like everyone else he would gather round, drink sly grog and swap yarns.

A noble person, Ernie Chapman was also a clever individual

whose survival and enterprising techniques were priceless in this new era. Just like his mates, he could turn his hand to almost anything. I often thought that if only this man acquired an education then we, the generation after, might have had an easier task ahead.

As kids, we could all see the daily disasters my parents and their relatives and friends faced. Life was totally uncertain. I feared growing up and wished Mum and Dad could be there forever. As I watched yet another of my new uncles being thrown into the police vehicle I would shudder. When I must eventually become a man, would the same thing happen to me?

Apart from Dad, Alec Menmuir was my hero. He knew everything about the bush and I followed him everywhere like a bad smell! To my benefit, Alec Menmuir was not caught up in world and Australian politics as much as the others. Rather, he was a cultural extremist. He told the old stories with such vigour and combined his storytelling with a hunting prowess yet to be surpassed in my experience. I loved that man. He led me, he showed me the way. He told me what I needed to know. When I failed, he took compassion on my beleaguered, inadequate, undeveloped body and mind.

From Alec too, I gleaned another attribute. He was an avid supporter of boxing and continually spoke of his idols. Joe Louis, the Brown Bomber, was his favourite and he studied and collected every piece of information on this gifted pugilist. He also mentioned other notable, professional boxers of that time. Heavyweights like Rocky Marciano, Jack Johnson, Primo Carnera, Tony Galento, Jim Corbett, Jack Dempsey, Max Schmelling, Don Cockell and Sam Langford. Other divisions boasted names like Sugar Ray Robinson, Carmen Bassileo, Dave Sands, Les Darcy, Freddie Dawson, Randolph Turpin, Jake la Motto, Vic Patrick, Ron Richards and Fred Henneberry. Alec followed the fight game with pride and the usual one-upmanship. But he did know much more about it than the other blokes.

Sickness

My brother, Ted, was the youngest in our ranks in the One Mile Gully home at the time and made his presence felt. Frail and prone to sickness, he counterbalanced all of this with his peculiar way of making fun. He was a happy-go-lucky kid, always pulling stunts on himself and others, laughingly disguising our miseries. I think he knew the world was stacked against us but he would not accept it. Several times, because of an illness unknown to us, he was placed in the old Wyndham Hospital. Often, his own fears welling to breaking point, he would run away from the ward and come back home.

Once, he was ill beyond measure, in hospital for days receiving medical attention. It was Saturday and I, with the usual grumbling gut situation, was forced early in the morning to visit the old tin outhouse. To my surprise, when I flung open the door, there was Ted, all of five or six years old, lying on the dirt floor of the lavatory covered up with piles of newspapers. Immediately I was afraid! I thought he was dead. As I stared in shock, a violent quiver shook his body. My heart went out to him. This poor, skinny, little boy, clad only in sloppy hospital pyjamas, lay huddled in deep troubled sleep, his chest heaving, his breath spluttering.

Many were the times I cried alone in misery. I did not want the others to see or hear me. I know that Mum cried those same tears a thousand times for us. The unknown was devastating. What would happen to us if Dad lost his job at the Roads Board? He was crippled now but was still expected to do a man's work regardless. We all depended on him. As we grew older and inherited the survival skills of our Indigenous ancestors, the bush would provide us with food. But that would come later.

Wandering Spirits

When night fell on our humble surroundings and weariness overwhelmed our tired bodies, we often huddled together in bed. We would sing or talk in the darkness, as one by one we drifted into sleep and dreams.

Now and then, a wandering spirit would come into our lodging in the dead of night. I could almost sense a difference in the room. What was happening? Why was I having this experience? Was it a manifestation reminding me of my traditional spiritual obligations as I made the journey towards adulthood? I could not sleep. I would lay awake in the blackness of the night, my eyes streaming with tears and tightly closed. I would pull the blanket up just below my nose. Even though my body was choking and perspiring, I still had to breathe. In my mind, the spirits were already in the room; hideous, wide-eyed, ugly. If only I could see them. Who were they? What did they want, and why did they come?

For thousands of years Aboriginals had been given reasons for such experiences and told how they occurred. Our people interpreted these visitations for those among us who did not yet know. I wondered if they were the lost spirits of those unfortunate persons buried in the cemetery less than a hundred yards away from our house in the Gully. There were more than sixty unmarked graves there, but only one wooden cross which bore a name: 'Vernon'.

Vernon had been a crew-member on the boat *Fram* from Forrest River Mission. There was an accident, a fire, and members of our people suffered a harsh fate. Some of the graves belonged to them. Mum and Dad had known them from the mission. We would occasionally place wildflowers and stones on the graves so we did not walk on them. 'Some most likely would have been traditional Aboriginal prisoners who just pined away and willed themselves to death,' Dad would explain to us. 'Or else they just succumbed to the hard labour inflicted on them when they built the bullock road over the hill between the Gully and the town. They had to bury them somewhere, apart from the European cemetery. There was nowhere else at the foot of the stony hills and they could not bury them between the work and the gaol, it would torment the others too much. Poor people.'

Much later, someone came along with a small D4 Caterpillar dozer, levelled the ground, and built two houses on the site. The spirits still mourn.

Back then though, I really was afraid. Not as much from the spiritual traditional owners of the land, but from the notorious Jarnbah. An ugly, hairy, smelly little muscular dark man, he was legendary. Every Aboriginal boy learnt of this demon-like creature who invaded your subconscious mind from puberty right through to old age. This aggressive, ever-present spirit being was obsessed with young girls and women. He was always jealous of young males in particular, and would present himself as the ultimate challenge. Over my lifetime, I have heard Aboriginal men from all over our district tell stories of their frightening ordeals with these ugly, overpowering creatures of the spirit world. They would appear and immediately want to fight. And the clash could be brutal and bloody, depending on your physical strength.

Whenever these traumatic invasions came, I would call out in the darkness to Mum and Dad. Having disturbed their peaceful sleep, I would receive a severe reprimand, then I would snuggle in close to my older brother. He never seemed to be bothered by ghosts. Had I inherited the legacy of my parents' Aboriginal spirituality which had been torn from them when they were stolen from their mothers in the bush? Had the spirit of the beings been waiting to again move in unison with the Indigenous life?

Sometimes I could match the Jarnbahs' powerful aggression. I would hit back at them with my clenched fist. They would fall to the ground, but always they would tirelessly spring back on their muscular legs, grinning hideously. There were occasions in these experiences with the Jarnbah, when they had total control over me. I would become conscious of being drawn down deep into the dark cavities of the earth, which I assumed to be their dwelling place. Here I would be at their mercy, limp, almost float-ing in this putrid, foul place. There would be many dark figures around, mocking, wide eyes glaring and force-feeding me with disgustingly foul smelling lumps of excreta, tadpoles and other things I could not describe. Every time, when I finally awoke from the ordeal, I would remember all the details but only have a very vague image of their faces. The foul unforgettable odour would still be there.

The stories I heard from others of such experiences were no different to mine. The many battles I fought and lost to these creatures that lived around us in the bush, I came to believe, were something all us young Aboriginals had to face and overcome. It was part of our growing up in this beautiful but harsh land.

Maybe, in hindsight, the inevitable had begun to happen. The spirit that our Indigenous peoples had sung about, painted on countless cliff faces and worshipped for thousands of years was now rejecting the descendants for daring to follow the spiritual presence that came with the white man. Maybe we ourselves were responsible for unknowingly reflecting the guardian spirits that controlled the thoughts of the Indigenous tribes as we gently trod the space allocated to us on earth. Maybe, in hindsight, the spirit recognised the defeat we felt.

Once there had been a two-way understanding of our Aboriginal spirit Dreaming. We paid a daily homage; by way of an acknowledgment, a ritual guaranteed our existence. Old women and old men dreamed dreams of life and meaning. They put them into song. It was the perfect world. Now, we are so overwhelmed by what is around us. I have not dreamed the dream for years. How sad! I mourn the loss of our Aboriginality spirituality. Maybe it is our fault? I am absolutely certain it is. We did not resist strongly enough so our young ones could know. Our culture was described by the English-speaking tongue as primitive, pagan, demonic, wretched and un-human, not quite the same as these supposedly privileged homo-sapiens. This was not a flattering view of a race of people who respected every natural element, every creature, and every boundary those same elements and creatures shared with us.

Early in my life I knew nothing of the powerful force of the various religions of the world. Gradually the effect of Christianity showed on my parents. It was clear the church was for 'good' people and not bad ones. To be good you had to be like them, the white Christians. Also quite plainly, I could see no spiritual effect, only a tokenism in the lives of the so-called good. The only person who displayed an outward attitude of their good was God's representatives on earth, the clergy or ministers of various religions. But as my life slowly dragged on, I became aware that even these persons had shortcomings in their responsibilities to their constituents.

What emerged for me was the fact that you could be good or bad, depending on what you wanted to be, and on your own personal commitment to your society. My experience is that I have not seen any such wondrous feelings of the peoples of the earth coming together in the name of humanity, peace and concern. So I can only be left with reality as it appears on the faces of people I come into contact with. This obviously tells me that everyone is a free spirit with no obligation towards their inheritance. Everyone except the Aboriginal, that is.

Ours is a spiritualism that has bound and committed, focused on the very essence that provides for the survival of our own humanity and existence. Still, I believe that every group of people that has existed on the face of the earth has had the same exact opportunity. Their own spiritual interpretation can contribute to their destiny. As Indigenous people, we were extremely lucky to live on an isolated continent with little outside contact until the last four or five hundred years at an estimate. Commonsense clearly points out that this isolation has kept our Indigenous spiritual focus intact. Other peoples have simply blown the opportunities as a result of congested living practices.

I mourn the loss of what should have been my Dreaming. Perhaps it isn't lost, just that I have never found it, and my search for spiritual intensity is lacking? Maybe I have only sensed that there is a vast capacity for learning? Maybe this is what I know as the Dreaming? Have I and other Aboriginal people missed it altogether? Or are we being provided with the first real opportunity to step over the threshold and embrace the spiritual beliefs that have been there all the time. Perhaps every person on earth has their own Dreaming.

Throughout my childhood, as a descendant of this continent's first inhabitants, often—and in the company of others, both adult and children—I saw weird lights glowing, moving. They were bright and dull, large and extremely small. I saw with my own eyes strange people moving about where there should not be; some people said that they were ghosts or the Jarnbah. In my youth, I believed that they were. There were min min, moving bobbing lights in the bush—I was astounded to observe this phenomenon even when I was wide-awake on a number of occasions. I may have been a dreamer; it is not for me to say. Maybe it can best be described as a challenge to further explore my own spirituality, a desire to acknowledge and confront the unknown.

Nowadays there are many interpretations and reasons for these strange happenings. Nonetheless, I still watch and wait hopefully for their recurrence. Maybe the fire and magnetism has gone out of this earth, however, and the spirits only revealed themselves when our culture was at its peak as it had been for those thousands of years. Maybe the new force was too great. How could we have foreseen the impending disaster that would tragically overtake our unsuspecting, inquisitive, unprotected spirituality? Did the peoples who came to these inviting shores capitalise on their own spiritual understanding and use this overwhelming power to bring the so-called primitive heathen beliefs to its extinction? History records that this is so.

Grave-Digging

To make matters worse, Dad was the local gravedigger, a permanent duty which went with his Roads Board position. Whenever there was a grave to dig, he would start as early as possible. The Gully cemetery was located on a shale drift off Mount Bastion's western front. If it was the wet season, the graves weren't too hard to dig. Most times Dad used a crowbar, a pick, and a shovel. As the hole became deeper, he found it more difficult to move in and out, especially with his stiff peg leg cupped over his short stump and secured to his left shoulder by leather straps. Most times he did not finish on time and was obliged to work into the night.

Mum would walk to the cemetery and take his supper over at sundown. Because there was no one to care for us, we would reluctantly go with her to the eerie old place of the dead and their tortured spirits. It was OK if we set out in the dying light, but when it got dark Mum would light the two battered old hurricane lamps and the scene would completely change. The evening sea breeze would cause the flames on the kerosene-soaked wicks to flicker. The moving shadows would play games on our minds.

Mum and Dad would work in turns in the hole to get the job finished. This left us sitting above the hole, staring into the limited light, afraid of ghosts who would surely be glaring at us from behind the tombstones. Big kids on the outside, little kids on the inside, we all squeezed together for protection. There was no squabbling here! Sometimes we played the game 'I Spy with My Little Eye', but nobody selected the letter 'G' because the word 'ghost' started with that letter. We did not dare to call them or wake them up. As the night slowly dragged on, the shadows flitted around. The metallic sound of Dad's tools of trade in combination with the eerie call of curlews and the shrieking of feral cats made us think that all the ghosts in the graveyard were calling to us. Only our parents could help us—and right now they were busy.

In 1949 we were about to begin our second year at Wyndham Primary School. Learning to associate with children from a different culture and pedigree was proving to be extremely difficult. Then, all of a sudden, a shock. The unintended passing of one of our little schoolmates. Kenny Fuller died, at just six years old. Up until that time I had believed, from watching my father at his burial job, that only old or sick persons died and had to be buried. Now came the reality. Children were not exempt from death; there was no rule that we had to grow up first.

Most of the children from Wyndham were present at Kenny's humble yet dignified funeral. I saw the tears and sorrow of Hector

Fuller, his wife, and their daughter Leslie, Kenny's sister. They were well known Kimberley identities, and the gathering that day confirmed the respect they were held in.

Wildlife

Porcupines lived on the Bastion Range and in the dry months would come visiting, in search of water. Native cats would play havoc with our domestic cats and sometimes kill kittens and puppies. Their frightening screaming would wake us in the night, as would the death throes of their defenseless victims. At one time or another we were all inflicted with nasty stings and other injuries from wild bees, wasps, beetles, worms, fish, scorpions, centipedes, flies, crickets, praying mantises, and ants. Every creature, it seemed, had teeth, fangs, claws, spines, fins or poisonous venoms and body secretions.

It was all part of our growing up and nothing really to worry about. Snakes were the real concern and in those days they appeared almost everywhere. But we became cautious from an early age, and learnt quickly to read the signs of danger and the injuries these creatures of the bush could cause when they were about.

When we lived behind the old Six Mile Pub in the early 1940s, we had many an experience with huge pythons and adders. One weekend, as a family, we went hunting. We set out early in the morning. A short distance from the shade of our camp, we came across a huge snake in the process of swallowing a small wallaby. I was not much bigger than the unfortunate victim!

Not all the creatures were threatening though. There were beautiful ringtail possums to be seen at night. Kangaroos and wallabies were in abundance; they seemed to sit under every shady tree in large numbers. Such an unforgettable sight! Goannas, if they dared, walked past our camp. They only had our dogs to fear. At that early age we could not catch them and had to rely on Dad and his rifle.

One day my older brother Laurie found a kookaburra chick that had fallen from a nest on a tree on the highest point of Mount Emu, the hill behind our house. It was a wonderful experience for us kids to keep this bird as a pet. It was a rowdy creature once it realised we were its parents and the only source of its food supply. We had no meat to spare so the local small bird and lizard population declined somewhat dramatically until someone's stray tom cat made his lunch of our pet.

Our parents taught us the old ways well. Bush tucker was everywhere; all we had to do was learn which time of the year various foods were available. We always had to bring the tucker home and share with the smaller children. I guess it was the law of the land, but we always ate our fill in the bush then took the leftovers home! Sometimes we cheated and ate more than our share, having seconds back at home. If we were lucky and speared many fish, we would cook them on coals and then stuff our bony frames. We vowed to each other never to let out our gluttonous secrets. But somehow, Mum always found out and told us stories of greedy boys, and of the starving millions in India. 'You must always share your hunt,' she said.

I never found out what India had to do with it. I could not imagine what any other country looked like. I assumed everywhere else was similar to our land: sparse of people, bush tucker everywhere. A fair share for all.

Home Duties

As the sun rose each morning behind the colourful Bastion Range we simply accepted the changes in weather and seasons.

Our activities focused on whatever was going on at the time, yet always thinking of our craving bellies and the home duties that had been strictly allocated by Mum and Dad. We carted all of our wood on a battered old wheelbarrow with a wobbly steel wheel. As our quest for wood slowly bared the surrounding hillside of dead trees at the lower levels, we quickly learned to ringbark, which saved us from climbing further up the steep, extremely rocky, spinifex covered hills around our home.

Whenever we were on our way home from school, hunting, fishing, Sunday school, anywhere, we had to pick up every stick, wooden box, bit of cardboard or old stump we came across. Everything counted. In the wet season, we had to collect special branches and stumps, green or dry. These were burnt to ward off the mosquitoes. It worked a treat, and gave us peaceful sleep.

Our old house had no fly wire on the doors or windows. These came much later, from Dad's foraging in the rubbish tips or simply acquiring them through light-fingered activities, some-times taking a cache that had already been secured by someone else's illegal means!

Smoke always burned our eyes. We didn't think twice about it. Certainly it never occurred to us that as our people grew older the gradual harm to the eyes from smoke could develop into a serious situation. Many of my people suffered back then, their eyesight affected for life, some even blinded.

Afghans in Our Midst

Our family lived for a while on the eastern side of the Four Mile Creek, near the existing township of Wyndham. The Afghans lived on the western side, adjacent to their mosque. (The foundations of this building are still visible today.)

Mum and Dad warned us of going too near the Afghan mosque. I do not know whether it was fear of the solemn, quietly spoken camel drivers and their unwillingness to mingle with Aboriginal people, or my parents' inability to understand the Afghans' cultural practices. They were always referred to as a separate people with a far-off culture and hence they should be left alone.

Many times the Afghans breached traditional Aboriginal protocol by trespassing on sacred grounds, right across the Kimberley. Who were they to know of the sacred spirituality of the Aboriginal culture? Like the Christians, they also thought that they were dealing with heathens, infidels.

Sometimes the Afghans took Aboriginal women, whether as wives or not. (As a result, a small number of our East Kimberley Aboriginal people claim Afghan heritage.) They traveled across the vast hinterland, displaying the captured Aboriginal women for all to see. They would have known full well that concerned eyes would be observing from the camouflage of the bush. Our Aboriginal people, from various tribal areas and station routes the Afghans passed through, would always know of the disappearance of young women. Our Law demands knowledge of their whereabouts for cultural reasons, and the bush telegraph would eventually reveal their location and often even that of the different Afghan groups they were traveling with. For their own protection, the Afghans kept their Aboriginal women in their swags as they slept each night—a sort of bush 'life insurance' as it were.

Few people now know of the sacrifice that went on. There are many lonely graves, consisting of piles of weighted stones to ward off dingoes, crows, inquisitive passers-by, and police. Whether it was a spear from the darkness of the bush or a cartridge from the revolving magazine of a .45 calibre early model side arm, the lives of many were taken as the Aboriginals tried to reclaim their women from being used as human shields. The Afghans were cunning in the measures they took to ensure their cargoes were delivered and paid for. Aboriginal lives were expendable, of no consequence to them, and if there was to be some sexual joy to be had along the way, so be it, what the heck!

With sunken eyes and emaciated bodies, those Aboriginal women would endure countless days on the march, transient, between deliveries, from port to station or goldfield, always awaiting release. The stink of the camel, its continuous slobbering saliva and sweat, the lolling gait as they tried to retain their balance and focus all day, flies everywhere, the experience was overwhelming in every detail. The sun was dehydrating, their eyes burnt with salty perspiration. During the day their saddle-sore bodies were tired enough. At night they endured the putrid, unwashed, weighted body of a male intent only on satisfying his sexual appetite. Calloused, unwashed hands took total control of the sordid act. Later, the thin, plaited, green-hide cord would be cleverly placed while the young woman slept an exhausted sleep, so any movement would alert the camel driver of her intended escape.

Sometimes one of the Muslim transport operators would become attached to his dark-skinned 'life insurance' and treat her with kindness, but such concern would be limited only to the particular poor creature in question. It's hard now to imagine the indignation that our Aboriginal people felt towards their women who, as mere adolescents, were kidnapped, thrown on the camel, and taken away. Imagine the trauma, the heartbreak, the fear, and the hurt. Although some of the young women would have been psychologically prepared for an early marriage ceremony according to traditional cultural practice, nothing could have prepared them for rape in the swag, far away from the main campfire, conveniently hidden behind the camel packs, cargo, and firelight. No one would have paid much attention to their muffled cries of anguish and pain. The next day, there would only be joking among the camel drivers and queries as to whether Allah had blessed his favourite son with a virgin or whether he had come out second best to an old, bearded, dust and fat covered bush buck with his hair tied on top in the traditional style. No thought or consideration would have been wasted on the young girl.

When I was a child in Wyndham, even though the era of camel trains was coming to an end and motor transport had almost taken over, the camel drivers still clung to their traveling existence. In 1948, our family met a drover with cattle and a camel herd at Sings Garden Spring on the King River road. An Afghan driver called Sik Anna was there and gave us rides on the camels at the dinner camp. I was extremely afraid of the beasts and howled when thrown up onto the camel's back.

Years later, the driver had the misfortune to be drowned on the Chamberlain River. But the Afghan must have anticipated the industry decline, having sold his camels to an old Australian roustabout called Jack Edwards. The stock work still relied on the camels because of the rough terrain and distance from the Wyndham meatworks. Eventually motor transport would take over. My father observed these developments, as history moved quickly, devastating in its consequences, and ruthlessly selecting its players as they were born. He was quick to pass this knowledge of his culture on for our eager young minds to consume.

Back at the Four Mile Creek, the Afghan mosque, a fenced-in timber and corrugated iron building decorated with Muslim religious emblems, defied both the locals and the elements.

'They worship a different spirit,' Mum and Dad told us. 'Something locked up inside. We don't know but they hide him from us. Look out! Don't go there, be no good for us.'

Shit Cart Run

Many times I pleaded with my mother, not to make me go to school but let me leave while my brothers, Laurie and Ted, and sisters, Rosemary and Helen, were still asleep and go with our father to help him with his work on the shit cart run. She knew I loved this ritual, and reluctantly took great pains to ease me away from the rigors of school responsibility. Some nights, just after my warm water bath in the huge galvanised tub, she'd say to me, 'Tomorrow, you can go with your father. Get up early, before sunrise. I'll wrap up a little damper and dripping and that leftover salt beef, so you will not get hungry.'

She alone knew that I always wanted to be with Dad. She knew how difficult it was for him when doing his job, to endlessly move in and out of the little truck, open gates and side entrances, in and out the back and front doors of countless lavatories in the township of Wyndham. It was hard for him with his disability to pick up the overflowing shit pans, carry them and place them on the back of the old Chevy 4 truck.

The mornings I was allowed to accompany Dad on his rounds, Jerry, our faithful old black dog, would make the effort to raise himself when he saw me up and about. He'd stretch, as only animals can, his tail wagging, before he casually strolled across. I'd be knocked off balance with his exuberant display of affection. He knew I loved him and would raise his grey brows, look at me with his dark brown eyes, asking for daily confirmation of my love. My skinny little arm around his neck, I'd be shivering in the early morning cool air, grateful for the warmth of his body.

Sitting on our front step I watched Dad with curiosity. The sun would still be behind the Bastion. Our newly purchased house in the Gully stood in the shadow of this magnificent mountain. The two parallel cliffs near the summit gave it the appearance of the fortresses of old, which was why the early explorers in the district had bestowed that name on this part of the Erskine Range.

As Dad got ready, the morning shadows concealed his muscular shoulders and slender but powerful arms. He tried hard not to make excessive noise as he went about his work preparation. The old Roads Board truck was parked on the slope with a rock in front of the wheel. If he could not start it with the crank handle he would let it roll down, engage the clutch whilst in gear and we would be mobile.

'Get on,' Dad would call to me, 'and watch carefully. I'll turn the crank handle a few times and when I tell you, push in the choke. And don't touch anything else!'

There wasn't much to touch on the old Chevy 4. I sat proudly behind the steering wheel and waited, my gaze fixed solidly on my father. Jerry would be keeping his distance from the truck, having already checked out the spoke-wheels and sniffed the smells that emanated from the many other dogs in Wyndham. The pungent aroma of human excreta still lingered in the pans on the back of the truck, in spite of the washing in water and a fresh coat of tar two days a week.

At usually the third swing of the crank handle the engine fired into life. Dad would looked at me urgently. I'd failed! The marvelous engine from Canada coughed, spluttered and died. 'Shit! When the engine starts, push in the choke, do you hear?'

'Yes,' I'd say meekly, as I slid lower in the seat.

Thank goodness no one was around to witness my shame. 'Shit!' I quietly mimicked his frustration.

Only my mother was there, standing silently. She would return to her kitchen as soon as we left.

I sat on a lavatory pan behind my father as he started his daily pick-up. The old truck chugged merrily along; there were no putrid smells now as I looked ahead with a feeling of importance. The front of the tray of the truck was the driver's seat and Dad sat on a piece of canvas folded to cushion the stump that should have been his left leg. He cleverly used his right leg to engage the accelerator and clutch and, when necessary, the brake too. On the dashboard, he had punched a hole and placed a handmade, number eight gauge wire, hand throttle. He could fix anything. He also had a remedy for the old radiator that constantly boiled. A simple piece of flannel tied on top would stop the globules of boiling water from blowing back into our faces. There was no windscreen.

Every house stop, every pan pick-up revealed something about the dwellers and their existence. Some of the outhouses were actually cathedrals, some clearly a place of convenience and reading, most just shit houses! Since we saw them from the unseen point of view, we understood the motives of the builder. Only businesses and well-to-do folk had custom-made out-houses. Most others stole, collected and made their construction material. At this early age I'd fast become an authority on out-houses, even though other kids teased me about it.

While our people kept, or rather, were forced to keep their distance, this line of work of my father's actually brought us in contact with the lifestyle of white men. I was intrigued. Some women in those elaborate houses saw my wretched presence and I suppose took compassion. They would see this skinny, shabbily dressed, barefoot kid, sitting among the pans. He must be hungry, and obviously needs care, they must have thought. 'Wait there, Cyppie,' they would say, 'I'll just fetch the boy some cake.'

They would come out with some exquisite portion, covered with hundreds and thousands, obviously a leftover from a child's birthday party days before but who cared. It did not occur to me then why they left the cake on the back fence post for me to fetch. I'll admit I was on the nose a bit and my hands were unwashed.

Other times, I hung my head in shame. Some white women, young and old, would severely chastise Dad for dragging me out on the old shit cart and making me work. 'That boy should be in school. He will never learn anything! I'm going to report you to old Goldie!'

Old Goldie

Old Goldie was the Roads Board secretary, a man in his sixties, defending his last term of employment. But to me, he looked like he'd just stepped out of an English history book, taken off his sergeant major's uniform, thrown away his yard stick and exchanged them for a neatly pressed safari jacket, knee length trousers and the equally impressive cigar that obscenely projected from the bristling mass of his tobacco stained walrus moustache. Dad never responded to the threats and taunts. Only he knew that Goldie was never concerned. His task was just as arduous. The Board had allocated to him just one corner of the huge wood and tin hall as an office. From there, he was responsible for maintaining municipal functions in this district.

Outside, a dirt floor verandah circled the building. He never complained because most of it was covered with two hundred litre drums of dingo scalps and wedge-tailed eagle heads and claws. Government doggers, station owners or just about anybody could bring in their bags of our native dog and exotic fauna and collect a bounty. It was Goldie's duty to ascertain their authenticity, pay up and live with the maggots and flies that were virtually everywhere in his office and building. This was why he continually cherished this huge cigar. He also developed the common weakness that European people living in the tropics somehow embrace. No one would find his bottles wrapped in canvas with the tops screwed tightly. His cache was hidden among the dingo scalps, tails and maggots.

Pans and Cubicles

As we progressed through the township, every business establishment was different. The Town Hotel was my favourite. In the gent's section of the lavatories, there were about eight pan cubicles and it was my job to race inside and check which ones were occupied. It was rarely used early in the morning so I would scamper in and peep under the swinging doors. I was not looking for feet but for lost coins, which occasionally were dropped by Wyndham's highly polished elbow benders. Now and then I would find the ultimate prize, the florin with the King's head, the old two bob. Not all the time would I tell my father what I had found!

Surprisingly, the police station had only one pan. There were always a large number of Aboriginal inmates along with the occasional white man whose crime would rarely be known by the town gossip. Seemingly, there was some degree of protocol among the gentry even in the Wyndham of that era. 'Thank goodness,' Dad said in answer to my question. 'They've made the prisoners carry their own pans and dump them in the gulf near the police station.'

Favourite Customers

All the prominent businesses and European investors occupied the eastern side of the main street on higher ground. The lesser mortals in the economy struggle inherited the lower ground and the foreshore. Here they would endure annual plagues of mosquitoes, snakes, flies that bite and flies that sting, floods, high tides, bogs, dead cattle and everything else that came down the Cambridge Gulf. But the Chinese population of Wyndham did not seem to mind; their ancestors had invented a remedy of some sort for just about every circumstance.

They were a quiet people, never appeared to be in the way of the bustling hillside colonial onslaught. Dad always told me that if the Chinamen left the goldfields it meant there was no gold to be found. He may have been right, but still they were quick to see the potential of yet another bonanza. The backs of their houses were oddly strange. Small rooms clustered together, elevated for obvious reasons and cluttered with numerous varieties of tropical fruit trees, vines, and plants in small garden plots. They all had chooks in makeshift yards and a cat or two patrolling the grounds.

The Chinese did not question the land allocations on account of them being seen as second-class citizens. Their ambition for the generations after them disguised any hatred that they might harbour against the dominant colonial culture of the day. I always wondered though, why their fruit and veggies looked so appetising. I was tempted to sample but the opportunity never came. Old man Fong Fan was always turning the soil when we came. Traditionally dressed at all times, Mrs Fong would busy herself in the garden with a huge homemade watering can, obviously keeping a sharp eye on me while their two sons Wing and Charlie looked after the business of shop keeping.

Others kept their eye on me too. 'That old Mrs Gee Hong Yet,' some of the boys would say to me, 'She blind, she can't see you.'

But her head followed my every movement when I went to check their pan. And she had every reason to watch me—they had the best vegetable garden in town!

In the mornings old man Lee Tong sat in the shade at the back. Late afternoons, perched on an old green wooden chair, he would observe the street's activities. I believe he did not miss a thing.

The Lee Tongs' youngest son Billy was our schoolmate. He befriended my brother Laurie and together they shared many adventures in Wyndham. Billy had two brothers, Jim and Tom, and a sister, Bessie, who shared the responsibilities of shop keeping and home duties. Their lifestyle was completely different to ours and behind their closed door everything they did was a mystery to us. Of these three separate families, the descendants of two still remain in Wyndham today.

The Chinese in Wyndham were Dad's favourite customers for one simple reason. They used their bodies' excretions as a valuable commodity and could not understand the waste of dumping it. Their pans were always extremely light on, and for this, Dad was eternally grateful. No wonder the fruit and veggies were top class.

Pan Dump

The first pan dump took place on the foreshore. My father would turn off the main street near the police station and cross the three-foot, six-inch gauged railway line. The little rocky road took us all the way down over the marsh and into the mangroves on the banks of the Cambridge Gulf. Here Dad would have to be very careful and drive slowly when crossing the train line. The rough ride could shake loose the lids of the full shit pans and the contents would fly everywhere.

The old Chev 4 was not comfortable to ride on at any time. There were occasions when we had to watch out for the steam trains that would pass from the Wyndham Port goods shed all the way across the causeway to the old meatworks' jetty. At the little jetty, two planks wide and about thirty feet long, we slid the pans and then emptied them into the water—or the mud, depending on the tide and its movement. I would always think that the catfish were lucky to have a free meal, but reminded myself never to eat one caught near there.

On our way out of town, we would pass through the Three Mile living area. Only a few pans to pick up at Bert Sharpe's, Drysdales', Cockings' and at Cole's. We didn't have to worry about old stuttering Bill Allyson's shop anymore. It had been abandoned and had just disintegrated overnight. Old Bill was always in strife with the police. The old coot was not gifted with patience and anybody who laughed, or mocked at his jittery attempts to be understood, was quickly clouted across the face. I was afraid of the man.

The Native Hospital

The next stop was one that would leave a scar in my mind forever. As we drove slowly up the stony road, behind where now stands Branko's BP Motors, I gradually shifted myself to a place of security, right close to Dad. Stan Legget came to the door of his comfortable home, constructed especially for living in the tropics.

When Stan recognised us, he immediately relaxed. He and his wife had the most difficult duty on earth, I thought. This was the native hospital and the only registered nurse, his wife, did all the caring for the afflicted among our kind. Many of us were still being born in the bush, but mothers-to-be who were having difficulties were brought here. Frank Chulung, who later became my friend, was born here in 1939.

The doctor would come on a weekly basis if requested and if the schedule in Wyndham town permitted. Meanwhile, ordinary illnesses and everyday wounds were claiming our people's lives at an alarming rate. But what shook my entire being and caused me to close my eyes were the scores of Aboriginal figures, standing or sitting and silently gazing at us. They were lepers. Clad only in neck-to-knee gowns, hands and feet bound in bandages, these souls had long ago accepted their fate. They were just patched up and made to feel better before the uncomfortable journey to Bungarun, the Kimberley leper colony near Derby.

Here, they would live out the rest of their days, slowly, constantly thinking of their previous lives, always wondering why, until their time came miserably. Even Dad took extreme caution because sometimes there'd be another dreadful job to be done after he'd finished his other task. He would be grateful on those days when Stan and his wife met him with the usual greetings and not the news that another dreaded thing had to be dealt with.

On those occasions, to my horror, quite unannounced, Stan Legget would be waiting. He would signal Dad to drive around the back of the hospital. By this time I would be doubled up on the front of the wooden tray, eyes tightly closed and head covered. Between the two of them they would quickly place the bundle wrapped in the grey and red-striped government blanket on the very end of the truck. They were both big men, accustomed to the task. Nothing needed to be said. The body was mostly always thin, stiff, and easy to tie down. Sometimes the feet were exposed and from time to time as I flashed a glimpse to see if the ordeal had passed, I'd see a part of a lifeless human limb. Those haunting visions of our departed Aboriginal people and the sight of the deformed and leprous feet have remained in my mind's eye since.

I clearly remember that Mrs Legget had beautiful auburn hair, in separate plaits that almost reached her waist. It must have been glorious to behold when she'd let it down. She must often have wondered just what she and her husband were doing in this dreadful place. Some time later, after Joe Mosey went south, they left and managed the store. I've often wondered where their son Jeff is and what his calling in life turned out to be.

The resource agency, Joorook Ngarni Aboriginal Corporation, whose board I founded and chaired, now occupies the premises of the old native hospital, and is still responsible for dealing with the harsh end result of the history of Wyndham.

The Six Mile Pub

Our journeys with the pans took us further out to the Six Mile Pub. This was always like coming home. Dad and Mum had worked here as yardman and washerwoman during the war years. We'd camped in a tent and bough shade near a huge bauhinia tree a hundred yards behind Arthur Bruton's pub. My brother Ted had been born under a tree in the Six Mile Creek one November morning in 1944.

I remember that morning quite clearly. Back at the camp, I could hear my mother's cry of anguish as she drew near her time. I had no idea what was about to happen; all I knew was that I had to help in her agony. Granny Mona Williams vaulted up, met me square on as I ran to the chosen place, a magnificent freshwater mangrove tree on the banks of the Six Mile Creek. She clouted me solidly and told me to clear out back to our camp a short distance away. Both offered no consolation for my childish dilemma. I was still confused when they walked back to the bough shade with this little whimpering creature that had amazingly appeared from nowhere. I would always be attached to Ted.

The Eight Mile Dump

The Eight Mile dumping place finally came up. A tractor-drawn grader had made deep furrows in the soft sand and all we had to do was tip the pans as Dad drove through. Most times he came back and shovelled the dirt back on top. This was easy. If the creek had water, we stood up waist deep and washed the pans and then coated them with a light bitumen mix. The pans were stacked on a rack to dry, and we reloaded the truck with previously painted pans. This site is still visible today.

There was no skylarking or just being happy with missing school, if Dad had a burial on his hands. This was serious business. No graveyard, no sign, no nothing. Human excreta was buried on one side of the road, human beings on the other. Dad crossed the road, dug a shallow grave, rolled the poor, unfortunate, unnamed Aboriginal person into the hole and, without ceremony, buried them.

If my brother Laurie happened to be with us that day, we busied ourselves in the bush or cleaning pans until Dad had finished his gruesome task. Most times I was alone and sat in the truck, facing the other way. I knew about Aboriginal spirits leaving the body. There were ghosts in every place, looking for people who had offended them in their previous life.

It did not occur to me then, but Dad must have had a stressful time burying our people. All of this, and alone, I wondered how he handled his own emotions. I never saw him weep. The faces of those he had placed so devotedly into the earth at the Eight Mile must have reappeared in all of his painful nightmares for the rest of his life.

Eventually, back on the run, I'd be overcome with pangs of hunger and thirst. The little dillybag of food Mum always gave us was devoured hours before. The water bag in front of the truck offered the only comfort: just scoop away the sugarbag flies, spit out the rest, and let it run down.

Going to Gaol

Without intending to, Dad managed to drag me into a new phase of his life. It started off only on pay days. His new drinking mates would all congregate at McCleod's pub, the Wyndham Town Hotel. They would say, 'A man's gotta do what a man's gotta do!'

I did not know what that meant. For me, it was hours of waiting outside the pub, sitting on the old shit cart in the daylight hours, then close to the doors under the verandah after the sun went down. My misery turned to fear and indescribable panic as Dad and his mates continued in boisterous enjoyment, never for a moment concerned about the vagabond kid now almost inside the front door. I was reduced to the same level as the many dogs outside the pub, waiting for their masters. The animals had a way of dealing with inferiority; I was alone.

My glistening eyes telling the story of complete abandonment, I waited hungrily for the moment I could glimpse sight of his wobbly frame illuminated in the brightly lit double doors. He would stand awhile, eyes becoming accustomed to the dark, then stumble across to the old truck. Normally it would have been a relief to be going home, but after Dad's drinking, the trip would be an ordeal never to be forgotten.

One pay day, Dad remembered the severe pasting Mum had previously given him. Although Dad never raised a violent hand against Mum, they had argued furiously. But they were married for life, no question about it. Life at this time in Wyndham was expected to be rough and sudden bursts of short-lived conflict occurred on a regular basis. This particular day was one of those.

My younger brother Ted had waited after school and was with me when Dad decided to leave town for the Gully. The old truck made its usual noisy departure from behind the goods shed in the old Wyndham Port. We were elated as we began our journey home. Mum would be pleased, and there would be minor luxuries in the home tonight. Unfortunately, none of these eventuated!

My dad had more to drink than he had bargained for. All of my fears came to a head as Dad stalled the truck directly in front of the police station. He lost control. The vehicle just lazily ran backwards off the narrow road and came to a jarring halt. As my father gathered his wits and checked our well being, the local cop, Constable Des Sculthorp, bounded across and severely chastised him. Within moments, Dad was arrested and locked in a prison cell. Des didn't know what to do with us children so he put us inside as well.

Naively, I thought our ordeal was over, but it was not to be. The policeman's wife objected to children being locked up. She pleaded and then shrieked vehemently for our release. After much reluctance on the part of her husband, we were set free. But we were now faced with another serious dilemma. In the drama, Ted had cut his foot on some broken glass. My shirt was the oldest and most dispensable, so I tore strips to strap his foot and stem the bleeding.

'You can go home now,' Constable Sculthorp told us.

Home was about one and a half miles around the Gully road. There was no moon or street lighting. We were frightened of everything the blackness of the night offered. Both of us cried all the way. Already feeling physically wrecked, I carried Ted on my back. Finally, after goodness knows how long, we reached home.

Mum embraced us and in tears asked what had happened. Between sobs we both spilled out the story. She calmed us, provided a meal and put us to bed. Little did I know that her own private misery was just beginning: there would have been so much that we at that young age would not have been aware of.

My father was released early the next morning. The old shit cart was still parked in front of the police station, pans askew, the tell-tale aroma wafting through the whole town. It was no wonder that after receiving a verbal admonition and being made to guarantee to pay the fine for breaching the traffic regulations, Dad was allowed to drive home. By this time, however, he was about three hours overdue for his usual shit can pick-up, and local residents had already started inquiring as to the whereabouts of Cyprian Birch.

Settled at Last

Ours was the first free Aboriginal family living in Wyndham. After all those years moving around the Kimberley after the exodus from the mission when the war began, we were settled at last. We owned our home and we had an outside water tap. As soon as he found the right sized galvanized pipes and fittings Dad would bring the water inside. Perhaps we might even have a sink, if someone threw one out. You would be surprised what white people called rubbish!

It was a life of luxury. We had a kerosene Tilley lamp for the kitchen and hurricane lamps for the bedroom. All the towns-people had their own power plants and electricity was a new commodity, but the bright lights attracted millions of insects and this activated the food chain for the creatures in every nook and cranny. I would shudder at the thought of huge brown snakes from the surrounding Erskine Range slithering through some-body's lounge room on the way to the chook yards. Lamps would do me!

Dad must have felt pretty good about his achievement. He had a job and new friends who obviously had a high opinion of him. 'Come and have a drink at the waterhole. You've got your citizen-ship rights now, Cyp old fella.' His white friends would say to him, 'Anybody say anything to you, I'll king-hit the bastard!'

They encouraged him to gradually overcome his feelings of inferiority. It must have been difficult for him. Perhaps he consoled himself with the thought that he did have obligations to this new society that had adopted him so quickly. Surely no harm could be done. After all, his father came from Scotland. There was fifty percent Caucasian blood flowing through his veins, whether he liked it or not.

My Dad spoke English as fluently as anyone on the streets of Wyndham in the 1940s. He never said so, but I know now, that it was his intention to prepare us for what lay ahead. Somehow he envisaged the difficulties our people would encounter as we strove for survival and recognition, although he would never know that in my lifetime I would come to play a major role in Aboriginal politics in Australia.

Whenever Dad noticed my emotions being shattered beyond all measure, his free arm would warmly close around my quivering shoulders. 'Are you all right, boy?' he would ask, not really wanting an answer.

I was his third child, and although the pecking order persisted within our family, somehow when Dad and I were alone, an uncanny vibration flowed between us. Yet the demands he placed on me as a boy, and later as a young adult, were enormously stressful. The answers I wanted were never there and many times I cried alone.

One Room School

By 1947, we were off to lessons. Barefooted, clothed but ragged-looking, we made our way across the salt marsh to the school at Wyndham.

The principal's name was Mrs Redding. She stood there, on the school verandah, looking at the rabble before her, conscious of our varied skin complexions and clothing. Everything we wore was a spur-of-the-moment imitation of how white kids dressed. Our mother had tried her best, but the patches were still obvious. Everyone of us was barefoot, except Rosemary, my oldest sister. Her flashing smile was her passport; her mature outlook would be our only hope for years to come at Wyndham school.

'Come on then. We can't hang around all day, can we?'

This was our introduction to education. The school was adjacent to the Wyndham Police Station. There was only one room. A huge blackboard dominated the front wall behind the headmistress' table.

Next door on the other side on the edge of the marsh was old Jimmy Neighbour's and Bluie (Edith) Lloyd's shed. Jimmy was a kind old individual but he hardly ever spoke. Anyway, who would want to talk with natives who really had nothing to speak about?

Charles (Mun) Bastian lived around the corner in another

steel shed. Most wet seasons, he would get flooded out with a combination of high tides and monsoon rain. It never worried him; his work was in town managing the Vacuum Oil Company's fuel depot. Norman Finlay, a Scotsman, his boss and agent, also owned the general store and gallon licence. (Years later, Arthur Vagg would obtain the licence and it has remained in his family to this day.)

Doug Davidson owned the next dwelling along. He used it to house the employees who periodically managed his store in O'Donnell Street. The last house on the east side of Wyndham was perched on the hill and occupied by the local taxi drivers, Jack and Beryl Whitton. They owned a beautiful black Humber Snipe car and everybody rode in that for every special occasion.

Every day we would walk to school, taking our time and enjoying the new experience. We met other children who lived in the Gully and immediately became friends. There was always a slight envy though for their bicycles, shoes and school bags. Ours were only flour bags with the 'Dingo' brand and numerous food stains. Paper wrapping around our lunches was rare, as first priority for its use was as toilet paper.

The Wyndham Meatworks had several senior staff members who had families in residence. Transport to school for those kids was provided in an old green utility that was called the 'Stinker'. After a while, we were accepted by these families and were occasionally invited to their parties. The names of children who accepted me I shall never forget and I proudly record them here for old times' sake. They are Jill, Ron and George Patching, Robyn and Louis Beale, Allan and Dianne Kershaw, Philippa and Ainslie Henderson, Karen Gasman, Ian and Janet Mansfield, Bob Casey, Ron Jones, and Rolfe, Finn and Ingrid Larson.

Other children whose parents had employment in the meat-works lived in the Gully across the marsh from us also became staunch mates and allies in our daily struggle. I also name these for the sake of friendship. These were Pamela, Allan (Curley) and Ross MacDonald, Jean and Rae Bently, Margaret and Maureen Smith, Ken and Bobby Johnson, Brian and Graeme Hyde, Steve, Kay and Owene Smith, Shirley and John Woodcock, Ernie and Billy Monaghan, and Joan, Frederick and Frank (Angus) Mills.

This last family had suffered tragically because their mother was of Aboriginal descent and the usual discretions of the day would come to the surface occasionally. The parents were evicted from the Forrest River Mission on the day of their wedding simply because of the mission policy that no mission personnel could fraternise with the natives. Mrs Mills was from the Gidja peoples, and was one of the stolen generations, a torment that would continue all the days of her life. Her husband, who I had known since my childhood, was a man of high morals and intelligence and retained this demeanor until his passing. The family still live in Wyndham and I acknowledge them as pioneers in intercultural interaction.

God Save the King

In our classrooms, early every morning, we would sing 'God Save the King'. The teachers told us he was the ruling monarch and everybody must bow to him. I could not see why. Especially since he was a white man from England and a million miles away!

I was completely confused. What was going on? I understood that Mum and Dad, in our Aboriginal way, were my superiors. After that, nothing! Except the cultural obligation.

Still, this bowing to royalty was but one of the results of the colonisation of our country. Caucasian conquerors had come with an intellect shaped by the confidence gained in previous conquests in India, Africa, the Americas, and scores of Indigenous island nations around the world. 'The sun never sets on the British Empire,' was on everyone's lips. At the time, I never understood the words. Now I know, may our Indigenous spirit help us!

The 53rd Boy Scout Group

My friendship with Alan (Curley) MacDonald developed as different types of opportunities came our way. He also lived in the One Mile Gully so, apart from him being non-Indigenous, we had many things in common. We shared most of everything we had and got on fairly well.

His father, who adults called Pat, was a gentle, quietly spoken returned soldier who worked in the Wyndham Meatworks. His mother was even more gentle and kind; she fed us continually with lemon syrup drinks, cakes and fabulously tasting titbits fit for a royal party. Mrs MacDonald's tropical garden was probably the best in town. But for me, it was just an overgrown jungle of plants and in all my visits I was constantly on the lookout for spiders, snakes and all other creepy crawlies.

Pat MacDonald was conscious of the town's many short-comings and took it upon himself to fill some of the gaps. He began bike racing for the girls and boys. This brought a lot more young people together. Later he started a boy scout group. We were in our element, decked out in a uniform. I moved to the rank of troop leader, with two stripes on my shirt pocket, all the scout uniform regalia and my first pair of leather boots. I was all teeth and smiles. There was only one problem: the long socks would not stay up on my skinny legs!

My day was to come soon enough. Her Majesty, Elizabeth II,

the new Queen of the British Empire and its dominions, was coming to Australia for her first official royal tour. Pat MacDonald, with his influence, had organised for two scouts from Wyndham to be flown to Perth to be involved in the celebrations of the visit. Curley and myself were chosen.

In April of 1954, we both boarded a DC3 Douglas aircraft and undertook the long, tiring journey to the big city where we would have a completely new adventure. We were separated in Perth, joined two different scout groups and took part in the marches, parades and festivities before Her Majesty the Queen.

I remember that I joined a sea scout group based on the Swan River in Midland. Mr John Everett, the scoutmaster lived a block away from the Midland Railway Station and cared for me all the time I was in Perth. Mr Everett and his father kept hundreds of pigeons and, like our Wyndham home, their place also had an outhouse at the back. I was in my element as it reminded me of home.

I had never seen so many people before in my life as I saw in Perth. Everything was awesome and I was breathless. Most inspiring was when the Queen drove slowly past and inspected our ranks, a sea of thousands of white faces. Then she blinked. One dark face among them apparently broke the monotony.

Still my socks would never stay up.

Many, many years after this, I met an Indigenous sister who had shared the experience. She was a girl guide, the same age as I was, and came from the south of Western Australia.

What I saw and understood in my travels early in life certainly did whet my appetite for the future. I owe a lot to Pat MacDonald. A true citizen of Wyndham, who actually got on with his life, he chose to ignore the negative attitudes among much of the society and concentrated on a more positive existence for all mankind. Mr MacDonald, I thank you for your foresight and humanity.

Much later in my life, I would meet Queen Elizabeth again. She and her husband were at a garden party at Government House in Perth. By then, I was well and truly out of my boy scout uniform, dressed immaculately for the occasion as a special guest.

We chatted and exchanged pleasantries about ordinary issues. With inner pride I had wanted to tell her about Wyndham and the bush but I failed dismally. My appearance, and the fact that I spoke English, confirmed I also was a constituent of the British Empire. Too late, the initiative lost. The Queen graciously moved on.

New Learnings

At school, the teachers noticed all of our personal efforts and told us so, publicly and privately. I loved singing and poetry and tried hard to pronounce words I did not know the meaning of. But while those early teachers were responsible for expanding my horizons, I really was not doing my best for them. Dad had already told me, 'That Aboriginal side that we have will always be with us, no matter what. We can never get away from that. No matter where you go, people will always know. What I want you to understand,' and he said this to me many times in my first twenty-five years, 'is that my father was a white man.'

He had never met him, but at least he knew something about him. 'His name was Edward Birch,' Dad told me. 'People in the Fitzroy Valley called him Ned. He used to be a mailman through that country in the early days. The road used to follow the river all the way from Derby to my country, Bunuba. I've got a lot of family there,' he continued. 'But I don't know them, only my two younger brothers, Edgar, Donald and a sister Nita. Like me, it's too late for them to shift back. We've all got family here and good jobs. There's only station work and I can't do that because of my missing leg. I have no money to buy an artificial leg. Never mind.'

The real truth would come out when Dad and I were alone together, and he was under the influence of alcohol. The issue was more deep-seated than even I could fathom. 'No matter what happens from here on, you are still half-white,' he'd say. 'Your other family is still in England somewhere.'

I listened because it was my duty, but still I did not have the faintest idea what he was talking about. 'All blackfellas out at Gundagai and Four Mile Creek, they are not our relations. Might be some from your mother's side but I don't know for sure. Listen,' he would say. 'You learn properly, listen to our Aboriginal people and you'll be all right. Try and understand what the whitefella's on about. This is the only way we can survive, I think. Look at what's been happening to this tribe around here, all around for that matter. Dying out from disease, being shot, poisoned, rounded up on reserves and missions. No future! I don't know.'

Every day, I hung on to every word of wisdom. I never knew what the connection was, but most days I found myself waiting for my father after school. One learning process ending, another beginning. Fridays in particular, he would be with his mates in the pub. As always, when he had finished his night of consuming alcohol, the traumatic events would begin for me.

Help at Hand

A new teacher, Stan Weir, had in a short time become interested in the social activities and experiences of Aboriginal students. His two children, Jan and Pel, quickly adapted to the Kimberley lifestyle and settled in.

One Friday evening, Stan was just strolling down Wyndham's main street when he came upon us in our usual predicament. On the footpath, opposite the old court house (now the Heritage Museum building), there was a small, wooden-arched bridge over the stormwater drain. This was always a trap for Dad and his wooden leg. He had stumbled, and lay bleeding from the elbows. I guess he went to sleep. Some time passed and I just sat close to his warm body for protection. It was late, no one went by and only the street dogs came, sniffed and continued on their way.

I was crying when Stan Weir came upon us. Dad was enjoying his inebriated snooze, and the concerned teacher took a while to get him sitting up so he could check to see if he was okay. This sort of thing had happened many times before. Yet again, Dad had broken the lower part of his wooden leg. Either he or his carpenter mates would have to fashion a new peg leg from bush timber or ballast pine. Another job to be done!

After much talk and repetition and more crying from me, Stan Weir left and then returned with his utility. We were taken home, only to face another ordeal in the form of my mother and more crying brothers and sisters. This however, did not last long and after hungrily gobbling down what food was left over for me, I collapsed on my bunk. Sleep came instantly but my brain would go on, repeating the haunting disasters and revealing the terrible sounds and visions of ghosts.

I wonder if Stan Weir ever got tired of doing this self-appointed task. Did he ever rebuke my father for his callousness and the neglect of his family on pay days?

Eleven years later in a church in Bedford Park in Perth, I was destined to meet up with Stan Weir and his wife again. Somehow he recognised me. I was almost speechless. This man had displayed so much concern and compassion for me when I was a child. I am eternally grateful for his acts of human kindness.

Parents and Citizens

Mum and Dad always made the effort to attend Parents and Citizens meetings at the school, but there were no real activities or recreation for us Aboriginal children. There were however, a few big events that the whole town took part in, exemptions being made for the presence of Aboriginal people. This, I guess, came about because Aboriginal children were allowed into government schools after the war ended. Once, we had the annual Christmas party in the Town Hotel, but all the others took place in the meatworks' hall. Other events included the fancy dress ball, Guy Fawkes night and the annual concert.

I had two sources of learning at the same time. Sometimes my schoolwork fell behind as a result of the traumatic occasions involving my father, and my youthful attitude soon shifted those aside. School was great and a joyful experience for me, especially when more and more Aboriginal families came to live in Wyndham.

Early in 1949 two other Aboriginal families moved into the Gully and squatted on Cockroach Hill as everyone had many years before. Other Aboriginal families lived on the edge of the marsh at the Gundagai area just a mile before the existing town site.

The Macale family consisted of Richard, the father, and two grown children, Ruth and Arthur, who lived on the hill adjacent to us. Alec and Elsie Menmuir came with their family and settled close by. They had a large family, the eldest being George. Then there were the girls: Margaret, Ethel, Jean, Lorraine, Dorothy, and Elizabeth. We became a close-knit group of Aboriginal families, sharing food, wood, clothing and just about everything else.

The job situation for men was improving. Other Aboriginal families were now camping at the Three Mile on the edge of the marsh and the Four Mile Creek, most experiencing the same dilemma as ours. Many came from the stolen generations with nowhere to go. All of the young women and men had married each other regardless of the mixed tribal situation and any traditional skin group requirements. Our mixed blood stolen generations were a new people, as it were, with a standard education and the chance to be competitive in the so-called 'land of opportunity'.

Cleanliness is Next to Godliness

Every morning at school we would have our hands and fingernails checked for cleanliness. The standard short back and sides haircut was the requirement. No excuse for the boys, or wear a ribbon until it was cut. We were disciplined with oleander canes for our many misdemeanors. We classed ourselves as lucky just being caned and then stood in a corner, or being paraded in full view of the classroom. We knew that Aboriginal culture was much tougher than this.

One day, another teacher, Mr Gilchrist, ignited something in me that until then I did not know existed. When he played his banjo mandolin as we all sang the national anthem, I was awestruck. I promised myself that I would learn to play an instrument—and I have kept that promise.

Cockeyed Bob

By late in 1947, the main body of the monsoons had not yet arrived. The searing heat was upon us, along with mosquitoes, flies and everything else that tormented us in their multitudes. All day the air was breathless and ominous signs were visible for all to see.

One day we had just arrived back from school and were tucking into the cake Mum had made. It was chock full of raisins, sultanas and flakes of ginger. As we ate the treat and chattered away, she sat sewing and preparing our clothes for tomorrow's school. The first rush of air was warm but was soon displaced by the congested dust and high cumulus cloud building up, the promise of yet another blow on the way. 'Oh! Come on you kids,' Mum shouted with urgency as she quickly got to her feet and looked out of the window. 'Hurry up and get that firewood inside. If it gets wet, you know what that means. No breakfast!'

We knew what it meant all right, but, not everyday—or year, for that matter—did we witness a dust storm of the magnitude of the one that was now rapidly approaching. It was just turbulently re-gathering itself after striking the eastern cliffs of the Bastion Range. A mile higher than where the lookout is, the remnants of the afternoon summer sun caught the boiling dust face to face and changed it instantly to red. We stood rooted to the ground. Would our old house in the Gully withstand yet another storm? We expected everything to be covered and packed with coarse gritty sand. Our eyes would be sore for days after, and we'd all have a lingering cough.

The dust was now catapulting over the brow of the Bastion and my mother's call was becoming more urgent. A deafening roar was building up, the mighty crescendo aided by the echoes from the surrounding mountains.

'Hey! Look!' we screamed in unison, our astonishment quickly mounting as there before us, a tiny single-engine aeroplane struggled valiantly to keep itself level and aloft.

The now increasing winds tossed the plane dangerously, sunlight on the wings and body revealing the fragile structure that was about to be completely overwhelmed by the darkening mass. We could not hear the plane now. It appeared to be slowing down, swooping down the valley, as if in an attempt to make a landing. Our hearts were in our mouths as we stared, spellbound at the dramatic sequence being played out before us, oblivious to the stinging sand on our faces. Then a new sound, the urgent revolutions of a single engine summoning all of its power. The landing must have been aborted. It was too late. The plane rose slowly, gathered pace and disappeared over the Cambridge Gulf and into the diminishing sunlight.

If we had any anguished concern for the people in the plane this was now forgotten. By now we were being literally hammered by the severe storm. My younger brother and sister were crying and I, a boy of about seven, wasn't doing a good job of concealing my terror at all.

With acute foresight, Mum had already secured the windows and doors with number eight gauge fencing wire. She dragged heavy wooden chairs in front of the two doors and covered most of our possessions with tarpaulins. The old house leaked like a sieve, we knew, and did nothing much to stop wind, dust or rain. Loose sheets of corrugated iron rattled loudly. Mum made us all huddle together under the huge wooden table. She had placed the coconut husk mattresses around this shelter in anticipation of the 'cockeyed Bob', which was on its way. She grimly looked up and prayed that the old rickety house would hold together.

The storm came and passed. It was all over by the time darkness was upon us. Mum flicked the dust off the table and wiped the second-hand crockery, and we had our supper. Dad, wherever he was, had to sit out the storm and then drive home later. Meanwhile, we sat and listened to a vast chorus of frogs—inside the house as well as outside in the murky night. Flying ants came in their millions and occupied every space around our only light. Uncomfortable!

But like the other people in the shacks in the Gully, we miraculously survived. A new day of bright sunshine revealed a cleansed landscape. The rain had given it a glossy look. The outhouse, however, had taken its annual knock. It had spread itself for about thirty yards downwind, but it was the only casualty.

The Flying Padre

Several days later the news came that the plane we'd seen was piloted by none other than our much loved flying Padre of the Salvation Army, Captain Vic Pederson. His many visits to the Kimberley took him to most outposts and on this trip I am sure he appreciated the presence of the Almighty! His effort to land at the Wyndham airstrip had been thwarted by the dust storm, which then followed him rapidly to the marsh in the Gully. His only chance to touch down was across the Cambridge Gulf. He had brought the plane down on a grassy strip, struck an unseen log and flipped the aircraft. Somehow he survived and set about a plan to reach civilisation.

As the story goes, after weathering the night's storm, Captain Pederson had breakfast, then proceeded to dry his clothes and equipment. To attract the attention of the small Wyndham settlement across the muddy gulf he lit a grass fire some distance away from where his aircraft had finally lodged. All was going well until the wind suddenly shifted, swinging in the direction of his camp. The fire quickly devoured the aircraft.

What a sad ending to a marvellous struggle for survival. Today, the burnt-out wreckage of the plane can still be found across the waters, a secluded and unsung epitaph to another part of the Kimberley's forgotten history. This man was responsible for bringing joy into the homes and lives of many isolated children. I remember him well. He had made previous landings on the marsh between the old port of Wyndham and the meatworks, so it was easy to understand how he had made his landing attempt in the emergency.

Once, after hearing him taxi up to the school in his small plane, we could not contain ourselves. We just burst outside and ran to meet him. To us, everything he did was magic. With a collapsible bicycle, a lantern slide projector, his expertise on the concertina and a captivating singing voice, he was the thirteenth disciple indeed! He talked about a God of love and caring, another culture, a better life. It was obviously important to him and I must admit it made me feel good. But how could anyone offer a better life than what we already had in Wyndham?

Lumpers and Looters

At least once a year, when the English shipping lines were in loading cargoes of meat, hides, tallow, and blood and bone fertilisers, the whole school would go on excursion down to the Wyndham jetty. The ships would sometimes stay up to three weeks, as the loading process was slow.

Under the management of George Constantine, gangs of men aptly called 'the thirty-five' would work up to twelve hours a day. These 'meat boats', as they were called, came from the United Kingdom and always had Indian crew. Once I remember we were invited aboard for the annual cake and ice cream party. We made friends on board and became a regular nuisance on the waterfront. The Indian seamen would feed us with the hottest curries and pappadums I've ever tasted. We would drink a gallon of water with every meal.

When Western Australia state ships came with domestic cargo we soon woke up to the newfound benefits. First there were the 'D' boats. They were the *MV Dulverton*, *MV Dorrigo*, *MV Delemere* and the *MV Denman*. Apart from the usual industrial-type cargo, they delivered frozen food and perishables to the many small ports along the Western Australian coast. Each region depended immensely on this supply base and the location of each town's port was vital. Each had its rickety karri pylon jetty protruding out into the sea. Wyndham had a deep-water jetty to accommodate the extreme rise and fall of the tides in the Gulf.

We knew the habits of the common 'lumpers', as the wharfies were then called. George Constantine, the wharfinger, was the only person to carry the title 'wharfie' in those days. That terminology would change soon enough when new loading systems and docking facilities were introduced. Meanwhile, the lumpers would give us leftover meat pies and sandwiches that were sent down from the Wyndham meatworks canteen by Joe Novell. In the period between ships coming to the port we would search the structure of the old wooden deck for dried orange peels and apple cores.

On pay days and weekends we knew that most lumpers would succumb to their well-camouflaged weakness and secretly sip away on amber fluids and at times more spirited beverages. As hours wore on, the usual seven metre plus spring tides quickly floated the cargo ships upwards alongside the wooden jetty. Continuous adjustments had to be made to the yard and middy (midships) booms that carried the usual single blocks and cables for hoisting the fast moving loading onto the jetty. This generally consisted of crates, bags and other quantities of stores for Wyndham, stations and surrounding district occupants.

Heavier lifts in that era were always prepared in advance by seamen on the ships and conveniently off-loaded when the tide was at its highest. Two winch men, plus the dogman or 'hatchie' from the shore gang, did all the machine operating. On some occasions, however, seamen drove the winches. But it did not take long for the Australian Workers Union Representative, Geordie Fagan, to get involved. He'd start shouting obscenities and union jargon in the thick brogue of his native Scotland. In those days, men squared off, clenched the fist and engaged in the dignified art of pugilism. This was always a high moment and we considered ourselves fortunate every time we got a view of a blue.

When the effects of carelessness or inebriation took over, and the men involved in the stoush lost their coordination, the cargo would go smashing onto the decks. Sometimes it hit the splintered jetty or fell into the muddy waters of the Cambridge Gulf. We would be waiting. At times the cargo lost would be crates of potatoes, oranges or bags of onions. We would casually follow the flotsam along the shoreline, as it drifted in with the tide. Then, as it came close, we'd swim out to retrieve it with the cord fishing lines we carried. Sometimes I would attach the line to my spear and use it harpoon fashion.

We knew that this cargo loss was never simply an industrial accident. Besides the meatworks' lumpers, local lumpers or casuals from Wyndham were periodically employed to handle excess cargoes of loose goods. These could be cement in ninety-four pound jute bags and two hundred litre drums of various fuels and oils. All of it was heavy. The casual workers were generally down and outers who had no real permanent employment. They had no qualms about allowing rope and wire slings, rope snotters, or cargo nets in transit to sideswipe the ships. They'd hit the bulkheads, the jetty's fenders and curbing, or sometimes the 'H' trucks on the primitive railway line, the required items spilling out onto the deck or into the water, to be picked up at leisure by their mates, stowed away and divvied up equally later.

Apparently George Constantine had eyes that took turns in being blind, depending on which side the 'accident' took place, port or starboard. People had to survive, one way or another. Whatever went overboard belonged to the scavengers lurking in the mangroves, and we got our share.

Some more adventurous lumpers went to extremes and actually took what they wanted off the railway trucks when leaving the jetty for meal times. The railway tracks were fixed in place on top of the wooden deck, and as it was difficult to safely drive on this surface, everyone rode the steam train and trucks back to the works when the meal breaks and knock-off times came. As they left the waterfront, they'd casually throw off a few boxes of condensed milk, canned fruit and meat, bags of chook feed and even cartons of blue label Kimberley beef destined for the international export market.

The opportunity would come later when, in the darkness of night, they came to collect their booty. Not all the time were they successful. We the unseen scavengers would again emerge to shift the spoils to our cache high above the watermark in the dense mangrove scrub. We left no tracks to follow and my guess is that the original culprits either never found out or just blamed each other.

If only they had taken notice of the smoke hanging heavily in the humid mangrove scrub a short distance away. If only they had made the effort to go and look, they would have been shocked. We had built platforms above the mangrove roots and the high tide mark. Wandoo was a prized hardwood and was already lying all over the place. Again the locals and maintenance workers just seemed to dump this vital commodity off the jetty for their own personal use. We would gather the timber and build our elevated shelters, hidden in the mangrove scrub. These places were our forts. We were really organised, partly on account of our

Aboriginal ancestry and partly from what we'd picked up in the picture shows.

There was a password to enter the location. We kept wax matches, a can opener, salt, cord to repair the spears, and rubber, leather and copper wire for the shanghai or slingshot repairs. We did not worry too much about water, and learnt to develop our physical endurance. As well as the necessities, we had our luxuries, the spoils of our imaginative war with the lumpers. When the tide was out and the mud too soft to walk on, or even when the spring tides were happening, we would sit in complete security and fill our bellies with new tucker. Always we would take stuff home. And Mum never asked questions!

We named the tidal creek 'Queenie Alice', simply because the remains of the workboat with that name had been dry-docked, abandoned and burned there. This creek is located between the north and south entrance of the current Wyndham jetty. The boat was used to transport all the pumping equipment and building material a short distance up the King River to the original location of the old pumping station. It also carried equipment to the construct markers for the shipping lane through the hazardous waters of the Cambridge Gulf. We would clamber all over the rotting hull and from one mud-filled cabin to another in our endless quest for live bait for Mum's fishing lines.

·Other· Things

When my older brother and other boys would talk with their so-called better vocabulary and greater knowledge about 'other' things, I was forced to listen. As the youngest in our little tribe on the loose in this big wide world of adventure, I was always the last in the single file on the hunt. I had to wait for my turn at everything, unless I was the scapegoat, the brunt of a joke or being set up for some dastardly deed.

One day, the oldest boy in our group, Arthur Macale, fell off a mangrove tree and ripped his trousers to shreds. The pecking order prevailed. He commandeered the trousers of the boy the next size down. This went on down through the ranks until I ended up in rags and near nakedness.

The many trials and tribulations of adolescence were not yet in my mind, and I could not fathom what the problem of the older boys was. Their 'knowledge' of things I'd never heard of or thought of at all seemed rather stupid to me. When I got to their age, I thought, 'I wouldn't waste my time.' But as time went by, I hung onto every word.

There were times when we played in the mud and swam with girls in Queenie Alice Creek. There was some truth in what they had said after all. My youthful body was restless, no end! As we waited for the tide to fill the saltwater creeks, the older boys boasted, giving vivid, dramatic impressions of what a young man's approach to a young Aboriginal woman should be. We would be subject to energetic displays, the emotion and physical action of which was mostly taken from snippets of the romantic movies of the era, or from stories passed on by older mates.

None of us knew how to describe the actual act of love itself. We only dreamed and imagined something that was as yet incomplete in our young minds. Each time one of our little hunting pack achieved the ultimate milestone, we'd all decide not to speak about our yearnings ever again. We would know without speaking that each of us in turn would acquire this maturity and be accepted in the adult world. We did indeed have a role to play. I do not recall any instances after 1955 of having intimate discussions about sexuality with those young men that

I grew up with. Another chapter had closed. The era of talking of such things among ourselves had passed.

The Pictures

Saturday nights were picture show time. Everybody in old Wyndham turned up to the meatworks' theatre. The manager, Mr Wally Ferguson, was a distinguished person. He and his family occupied the best seats in the house. After that, the meatworks' heirarchy prevailed. Abbie Woodgate, next in charge, occupied a place of prestige with his lady friend. A senior person in the meatworks' office, Digger Geddes, also enjoyed the privilege of a good seat. There was Bill Flinders and his wife, Doug Davidson's family, Fred Ryle the Flying Doctor radio operator and his wife, son Jim and daughter Jennifer.

Of course in those days, we knew no adult white people by their first names. Everybody was Mistah or Missus, and they all called us Boy or Girl. Nonetheless, I saw what was going on around me, and the seating arrangement at the picture show told the whole story. We, the underprivileged natives, sat in front on the dirt floor along the side walls; we might have gained free entry but we also acquired stiff necks from the night's proceedings.

This was still very much the colonial era. The state government was looking for new options in the Kimberley because the notorious plight of Indigenous people was attracting national and international attention. Unfortunately, any developments were at the expense of the Aboriginal people; we were still being exploited and were doomed to remain second-class citizens for many years to come.

Gamblers and Boozers

I used to hear my dad and Uncle Donald speak of the spinning ginny and the small fortunes that could be made if you were lucky. Gambling was rife amid 'A' and 'B' quarters when the meat-works' season was in full swing. Workers used to hide money in mattresses and cardboard boxes. Businessmen in Wyndham—like Charles (Mun) Bastian, Jimmy Neighbor, Wing Fong Fan, Norman Finlay, Jimmy Lee Tong and Billy Flinders—would bet heavily at roulette or dice, or at the weekly two-up school.

Small fortunes were made and lost at Norm Dixon's unlicensed gambling venues. First the publican, McCleod from the Wyndham Hotel, then eventually Silver Fox (Des Gee Senior) would take crates of bottles of the wondrous amber fluid around to the living quarters on the Wyndham Meatworks or up to One Mile Gully to quench the thirst of their many clients. The grog was delivered by an Austin truck known as the 'Bum-boat'—because most times people asked to have their purchase put on the slate until Friday, otherwise known as bumming off the publican. The ritual would bring many a good man down and I guess many letters of explanation were sent to scores of diligent, patient wives waiting below the twenty-sixth parallel for the vital income.

Drovers

Come April or May, the weather changed and it seemed every crea-ture came to Wyndham. With the cockatoos, the drovers and cattle arrived. Before our time, the meatworks had built a delivery camp ten miles away, at a place known as Chimoolie. In earlier years, they employed an on-site manager for the full season, and possibly longer. A huge dam was built and there was a house, water wells, horse yards and a concrete watering trough. The telegraph line extended from this point all the way into the meatworks near the sea.

Every morning the man on the job would climb the gnarled old boab tree using the steel spikes and discarded horseshoes that had been driven into the soft pulp of the trunk. From this vantage point his eyes would search the eastern horizon for moving clouds of dust. A mob of cattle would be nearing its destination and could be just two days away from delivery.

After making his estimation of distance and calculating their time of arrival in the meatworks' paddock at last camp, he would carefully lower himself to the sandy ground then pass this information through the telegraph to the meatworks' stockmen.

On delivery day, usually at daybreak the tally would be taken by the boss drover and Frank Pober, the meatworks' head stockman, as the cattle made their way through the double gates at the western end of the holding paddock. When the final tally of the herd was complete, the drovers would ride past our school.

Somehow Mum and Dad always knew the names of the drovers who were passing through. They spoke of Aboriginal people we had never seen before. But we knew of them, we knew of this amazing kinship connection, of genetic features within our families; we knew what and who to watch out for.

July Oakes, according to Aboriginal Law, was my first cousin. When he first came to Wyndham he observed the Aboriginal custom. He stopped first at our home in the Gully and showed respect to his aunt (my mother). He had not known my mother before, but the Mirriwoong/Marlngin protocol demanded that he make himself known. He was the first person to inform my mother that her mother, Granny Boonay, was still alive.

In years to come, this extremely handsome man with an

awesome physique and an intellect to match, would become the first Aboriginal in the East Kimberley to represent our people at the national level. This was in 1973 when the Commonwealth Government created a precedent whereby our Aboriginal people elected representatives in thirty-six regional councils throughout Australia. (Known as the National Aboriginal Consultative Committee, it was the forerunner of ATSIC, the Aboriginal and Torres Strait Islander Commission.)

Prisoners

All I had to do was sit down and wait. It was his bike. A beat up old Malvern Star. Laurie was eighteen months older than I was and his glare told me if I stepped out of line, I would endure misery no end. I waited. Hopefully, he would soon be tired of riding around the marsh and come back and give me a ride.

To my amazement, he suddenly stopped his antics and came directly towards me. 'They're coming,' he cried out. 'Big mob, this time. Come out here, you can see them better.'

I knew straightaway what he was referring to. My turn on the bike was not going to happen. I got up and walked out to the edge of the marsh. It was a familiar sight. There, about three hundred yards towards Wyndham town, the local police constable was leading the single file of Aboriginal prisoners, the black tracker bringing up the rear. There were about twelve or thirteen, all walking free, barefoot, baggy trousers, no hat, and no shirt, glad for today's excursion up the Bastion Range. Both policemen had lever action .32 calibre Winchester rifles, with a tube-fed magazine below the hexagon barrel, effective for hunting wild goats on the rugged mountain before them—or for dealing with any other matter.

I placed myself conveniently on the big rock near the road as they silently came towards us. What was happening to these black people? Why were they in gaol? Were they the murderers we had heard about? Dad and Uncle Alec had said that they had heard that the mounted police and black trackers had brought up another mob from Menmuir's paddock area and Karunjie Station. They were cattle killers and under Australian law had to be punished. The whitefellas had taken up all the land now and black people had no right to kill their cattle. If they wanted to avoid trouble, they had to walk onto the missions and hand in their spears.

This day the prisoners made their journey up the face of the Bastion to the cliff. Here they would ambush the feral goats that made the daily journey to the western side for the comfort of the early morning shade. Then the policemen would shoot all they would need. The prisoners would carry the carcasses, skinned and gutted, in a piece of cheesecloth or a strong hessian bag to protect it from flies. Back at the prison, the goat meat would be salted and dried.

It would be mid-afternoon by the time the prisoners returned. Hot, sweating, covered in flies, no doubt they were glad the ordeal was over for at least another fortnight. As they shuffled past us, only a few would offer a flash of glistening white teeth. All of them, young or old, had magnificently proportioned bodies beneath their shabby attire. I could see the traditional mutilations shining starkly on their upper torsos as they walked past us in the sunlight.

Dad told me that when they went to hunt goats, they would have their last drink of water at old Percy Frank's shack at the base of the hill. The old-timer loved this and always used the opportunity to frighten the prisoners. He apparently had roamed the bush years before. With his humped back, scraggy, nicotine-stained face and the six shot .44 revolver he waved about madly, he could set anyone's mind off. Us kids used to wait until he got stuck into the rum and then tease him something awful. He would chase us and fire shots into the air.

When the white cockatoos descended on the Wyndham Meatworks in their thousands, we knew the season was changing. They'd come winging over our place at dawn. Noisy creatures!

The new season meant that the policeman—and anybody else who had transport—would throw a couple of bottles of rum and a cheap bottle of plonk in a bag and drive out to droving camps, as far as the bend of the Ord River (Carlton Crossing), or the Twelve Mile Billabong. Here they would ask their drover mates for a clean skin killer. Somehow they always anticipated that there would be stray cattle, and it was easy enough to deal by bartering. At least it meant the prisoners would not have to climb the hill again until after the meatworks closed in September.

Our school stood next door to the prison. There were numerous holes in the high iron walls and we could see into the yard. We relied largely on our imaginations as to what went on inside until the day I went in with a mate to visit his father, who had been gaoled for six months. I was shocked. The main prison cell was a huge room made of rock and concrete. At regular intervals, there were steel rings concreted into the floor, obviously to secure hardened criminals. Once locked in, no one could escape the place. Ordinarily, less troublesome inmates camped together at the front entrance behind the huge bars and swinging steel door.

At the other end, to my utter dismay and extreme shock, were many four-gallon open kerosene tins filled with human bones. Bones and skulls overflowed and were stacked in one corner. This was a place of torture. How could anyone sleep in this place? Were the piles of discarded human bones just collected police evidence? Perhaps no one cared a stuff about the Aboriginal inmates anyway? Many people didn't even consider us to be human beings, so what was the big deal? Or had the punishment been designed to break our people's spirit?

In the bush, dealings with death and bodies and bones were commonplace, but controlled through ceremony, over a period of time. Here around the Wyndham area many tribesmen, women and children, had virtually disappeared off the face of the unforgiving earth. These bones could have belonged to them. There was a right time to mourn, a right way to view skeletal remains, I thought. This was a cultural disaster.

Outside the prison cell in the yard was a large concrete block. It was about knee high above ground level and had a steel ring in every corner. One day, I found out what this was for. It was in 1950, just after my youngest brother Leonard was born. He was the only one of us born in a hospital and when Mum was leaving the hospital she went directly to the police station to register his birth. I was with her, nervously standing near the door, bad memories racing through my mind. The policeman's wife was talking to us while we waited for him to attend to us. Suddenly we heard a male voice in obvious distress, shrieking loudly. Immediately, the woman ran out behind the station and screamed at her husband to stop flogging the unfortunate individual. In her haste, she neglected to close the door and to our utter dismay we saw what was actually happening. These acts were a common event in Wyndham in those days. We left quickly.

The Stock Route

The live cattle-loading facilities were still intact after the war in spite of the old jetty having burnt down. The holding yards and the cattle dip were on the foreshore. A protective fence made of thirty-five pound railway lines to stop cattle escaping, extended from the holding yards all the way to what was called the bullock road.

This land feature still exists and is about a mile east of old Wyndham. There was no space to drive cattle through the township. To get them around the Erskine Range would take another two or three days' droving. The solution was to build a shortcut stock route over the range between Mount Emu and Mount Albany. Aboriginal people were readily available, so the labour situation was not a problem. In stories passed down to us we heard often that 'big mob blackfellas been move all that rock for that bullock road'.

The construction took place under police guard. One policeman and one black boy watched the Warriu* (east) side and another policeman guarded the other side. All guards had lever or pump action rifles and guns. It must have been sheer hell for the scores of Aboriginal prisoners, fretting their lives away in full view of their traditional country all around. Bare feet, heads and hands, all never before experiencing this sudden stress to their bodies. It appears some, being free of chains, may have attempted to escape, or some just succumbed to the unnatural physical pressure placed on them. We do not have a clear story but the evidence is there. The stock route verge is piled with all sizes of rocks, the walls up to three metres high in places. Some effort!

One time, myself and several other boys came upon a pile of human bones and skulls under a cliff face shelter up there in the Gundagai Valley (now the Telecom tower area) adjacent to the stock route. It was no burial ground. We ran for our lives in sheer panic. Years later I returned to check and found that all the bones had disappeared.

Commencing at the Three Mile near the old rifle range, then going straight up and then straight down, the route was short.

*Aboriginal name for the Bastion Range.

The first herd every year turned the path into powdered dust and a cushioned walkway.

The Afghan camel drivers had also built their own path for their animals but this was only a metre wide. As was their custom, the camels moved in single file, attached by nose pegs. This path can still be seen adjacent to the bullock road over the hill and also crossing the Erskine Range behind the Seven Mile cemetery.

The Wyndham mountain stock route was not the only one. The Duracks from the famous Argyle Downs station settlement did exactly the same thing. At a place now called Durack's Folly, history records they executed a feat of enormous engineering proportions. No mention is made of the Aboriginal sacrifice. Similarly, at a place called New York Jump-up, on the old Karunjie road, a path had actually been carved and built out of the mountainside with forced Aboriginal labour. This Aboriginal history has only been recorded by word of mouth. What was passed on to us is this: 'Blackfella been work! Been runaway, been die, all over Wyndham country!'

Such statements clearly confirm the use of Aboriginal slave labour even in the construction of the foundation of Wyndham town in the old port. This is evident too in the huge excavations from the hill behind the town. The town does not sit altogether on a natural peninsula, so when heavy haulage passes through the main street everything on the west side, in certain sections, shudders. It is similar to an earth tremor.

Wunan Trading

Whenever we saw the Aboriginal prisoners under police guard so close to where we lived, we had some means of contact. We picked up their strong musky body odour, dry, but still distinctive, early in the morning. Each time I would be immediately transported to my first contact with tribal people at our camp behind the Six Mile Pub during the war years. Bush people who had not been seen ever by white men, they would come early in the night before the hotel's noisy old power plant was shut down. They were afraid of the white folk who were known to mete out severe punishment for the killing of their prized beef cattle, or even for daring to stand up and confront those who callously, unashamedly trespassed on sacred land.

Before the tribal people came our way, our parents would see the message in the sky for weeks before their actual arrival. They kept us informed as they plotted their daily course with small bushfires on the route taken by their ancestors for thousands of years. It was different when the police patrols were assisted by equally clever black trackers, or police boys brought in from other states. Our people would retaliate, take precautions. A skilled tribal man would bring up a rear guard, as it were, one or two days behind. Using wind and smoke he would checkmate them. Perhaps somewhere in days to come, they would seek vengeance against their devious blue-eyed pursuers.

The tribal people were well prepared for their visit to our camp in the blackness of night. On picking up the scent of guests, our dogs would bark, although they remained absolutely quiet or resorted to a frightened quivering when the presence of the bushman's dingo came wafting in with the gently cool winter air.

I was always glad when they came. They brought coolamons and large dillybags filled with all sorts of bush tucker, gathered and cooked on their journey. The large sea mullet and barramundi wrapped in paperbark were an extreme delicacy and easy to collect. Courtesy of the Japanese bombing raid on the Wyndham airport, there were huge craters around the mudflats and closer to the King River. When filled with tidal water they contained a variety of edible fish and the local Aboriginal people competed fiercely with hundreds of squawking pelicans and countless other hungry creatures. They would block the tidal creek with mangrove limbs and branches reinforced with clumps of spinifex brought in from Boola-Njee (Flapper's Hill) before the saltwater receded. A covering of paperbark floating on the water immediately downstream below the trap would ensure that any fish leaping over the spinifex would not reach the safety of the saltwater. Any large fish that thrashed through the gauntlet was quickly speared. The rest settled in the bomb craters to await the next tide.

A special type of mangrove tree grew on the main river system. Short, manageable lengths were cut and carried to these small estuaries and bomb holes. Then everyone would move into the water. Children would splash around happily while adults began stripping the bark off the prepared saplings. The sap was white, milk-like, and after some time, it started to affect the fish within the isolated pool. The substance hindered the fishes' breathing and they came floundering to the surface only to be speared or bludgeoned with a stick. Happy days!

Dad had a standing bargain with the tribal people that he always honoured. In the period since their last visit he would have accumulated a reasonable supply of nicky nicky (tobacco), cloth, canned foods, sugar, salt, treacle, tea and flour. He also went to extremes to collect any available pieces of steel. Our bush people placed a great priority on these as they moved from the Stone Age into the Iron Age. Their new steel-tipped spears (shovel spears) proved to be deadly accurate with the enhanced weight and extended sharpened blade. A new image of power for the so-called noble savage was struck.

The Loombia Story

Years earlier, Loombia, an Aboriginal elder from this very tribal grouping, had used the infamous shovel shear to dispose of his mortal enemy, Frederick Hay from Nulla Nulla outstation on the Forrest River Aboriginal Reserve. Hay's lust for young adolescent Aboriginal girls had brought about his undoing.

The story I have known all my life tells that, while riding around the property and checking stock from 'marauding' Aboriginal people, Hay came across Loombia and two women gathering lily pods and stems in a billabong. The situation was too easy to pass. Before Hay went about his dastardly deed with the younger woman, just for good measure, he flogged Loombia with his stockwhip and left him at a short distance, bleeding and painfully drained of his traditional authority and any thought of retaliation for the moment.

However, Hay's lust and sense of determination must have lulled his brains momentarily. He did not want to kill the old man, just keep him off until he had satisfied his lonely desires. A bit of booze, a bit of young black velvet, money in the bank when you hit town, your own law. Shit! May as well indulge. No one will know! These bloody savages can't even speak English! Who are they going to tell? Father bloody Gribble?

Hay took the usual precautions even though he anticipated a quick interlude. He stripped off everything except his boots, then for a moment was lost in his own desires. By the time Loombia became fully aware of the events that had just passed, Hay was already finished. He noticed Loombia's approach, grabbed his clothes, hat, and stockwhip and as good as naked swiftly booted the stirrup, and mounted his horse. 'The old bastard has got a bit of fight left yet. I'll give him something to remember me by,' he muttered.

Too late, he realised, as he nudged the stockhorse forward, that his rifle was still in the scabbard on the saddle. And even though the whip was stinging the air as he approached the ancient warrior at a canter, nothing could stop the shovel spear in full flight.

Loombia had barely finished removing his prized steel projectile when the crows and fork tail kites started and circling overhead. He covered Hay's naked body with leaves and branches and with burning hatred turned away swiftly.

Later, much later, if time permitted, he would deal with the ngarli (young woman). She hung her head, cleverly not showing her emotions, standing a short way away then following at a respectful distance.

Not a word was spoken as they gathered their meagre belongings, some food and moved to stony ground for security. They would walk long into the night. Tomorrow they would change direction towards the new glow they saw in the evening. There would be relations and old people to console the fugitives. The people must be warned. A white man has been killed. Beware! Do not follow the hunting paths—and do not go to the usual wet weather meeting places.

Kimberley Legends

Kimberley Legends

Me and Barney

I've been a stockman, long time
Can't remember how long for sure
Barney and me were young fellas
Back round 1934
Stories no different to other blokes
Who worked in the Kimberley that time
It's just that I was born in my Dreaming
And he from another clime

Remember Barney, the ringers
Around the stock camp at night
Telling old yarns with laughter
Till last watch when the east was bright
The cold weather smell of horses
When moving around the herds
Gave senses a tingling reminder
While we sang of different worlds

The damper and beef was good tucker
No shortage of tea from the cook
He knew how to fill your binji
Nobody lazy, frightened to work
Remember the old boss drover
Short, tough as desert oak
His only true love was a knuckle-up
Of women he seldom spoke

The rain sometimes in cold weather
Shook your guts and your bones
I think Barney, old stock mate
It's a wonder we're alive back home
The going was tough and bitter
God knows I cursed those days
Slippery and Jack are gone now
We follow them soon same way

Where are you now old fella?
Been years since we had a yarn
New boss say you're in Queensland
Old and still on your own
Me, I live with my old woman
Pensioner, crippled and we finish
Reserve got nothing but problems
Oh where that good life we wish

I am not proper happy
Old memories get me down
You know what I want old Barney
We were still workin' around
I don't suppose we'll ever
See them days again
No more room for old blackfellas
Who only talk of times that's been.

The Pipeline Cowboy

The water supply pipeline passed behind the Birch house at the base of the range of hills. It followed every land contour, all the way from the King River pumping station. The survival factor was strong. People used every available bit of land adjacent to the cast iron pipe.

Australia was a land full of squatters and jacks-of-all-trades back then. Everyone selfishly tapped the line at scour valves or joints, helping themselves to the precious commodity. Years later, these dwellings would become legal tenures and form the basis of a new suburb of Wyndham. At that time our family lived on Cockroach Hill, while a so-called elite among the squatters occupied the One Mile Gully across the salt marsh.

The pipeline was continually checked for small leaks and ground erosion. Basic repairs were carried out by an old chap called Bill Hurst, more commonly known as the 'pipeline cowboy'.

Old Bill was of huge proportions, reasonably tall with the full belly of a Kimberley pioneer in his latter life, just dodging the pension. Everyone always wondered how he managed to fit into the old, shining poley saddle, let alone slip on his polished R.M. Williams riding boots.

He carried out his endless job without complaint, riding an ancient draughthorse. An even older one on a halter lazily meandered along behind, carrying his swag, supplies and tools of trade. If Bill found a leak—apart from the usual ones behind shanties along the line, which he ignored—he would carefully drag himself off his faithful standing horse and set about his not-too-difficult task.

Bill would light a fire in the shade, if a tree was available. He was the master of job presentation and non-exertion, and we watched his every move. It was he who had taught us how to ringbark trees close to the known leaks that he had to patiently re-pack time after time, year after year. But the shadiest trees were always left untouched and, nurtured by the blessing of regular horse droppings and the surface soil being kneaded and tilled by massive but gentle hooves, grew well. While Bill set about his task, the old horses walked on the spot, quivering in their efforts to avoid the bothersome flies.

Extreme heat in the tropics caused contractions in any metal lying on the surface of the baking ground, so old Bill's work was stifling. He'd squat or sit on a thick hessian bag he carried for just that purpose. Over the fire, he melted enough lead to pour into the joints to seal the break in the pipe and stop the precious water leaking out.

Elevated tanks at the King River, along with several booster pumps along the way, guaranteed the water flowed efficiently. The last pump in the Gully had a huge, noisy diesel engine, which lifted the precious water up into the large concrete storage tank above the Wyndham Meatworks on the side of the mountain.

Old Bill carried the lead in sheets in his saddlebags. He would cut the metal into strips and place them in a steel pot suspended over the fire by a small steel tripod. It looked like he was cooking something to eat and us Birch kids would hang around, testing the breeze for food smells. Old Bill Hurst was not interested in small talk with the little nuisance darkies, but he always grunted an acknowledgement when we were near and watching. And we were almost always there. Sometimes, surprisingly, he would question, 'How's your old man, Cyppie?'

The bravest among us would chirp, 'Good!'

It seemed to satisfy him. Although it bothered him to talk and to take his old bent pipe out of the gnarled old mouth, there was no bitter twist in his ancient features, nothing that displayed any animosity. Apart from his pipe, the object he cherished most, Bill had one other luxury. The bottles were carefully wrapped in the saddlebags to prevent breakage and the telltale sounds of tempered glass. We never saw what they contained, but there was the strong odour of whisky or rum besides tobacco.

The first part of Bill's journey from the Wyndham Meatworks to the old Six Mile Pub was unhurried, routine. Mostly this stage of his responsibility was carried out by Gully dwellers, and others who just bludged on the system to provide water. When he had completed his job he would casually place his gear back in his packs, speak kindly to the patient animals, and suggest they wait a little while longer.

The old gooseneck pipe would appear in his mouth. He would fondle around below his protruding belly, fingers moving along his second belt to retrieve his stockman's pocketknife. Then he'd cut off the appropriate proportion of tobacco, reminiscing as he did so about when he last used the chosen blade. Maybe it had been to cut a young bull calf's testicles from its sack. The tissue gleaming white under the skin, the fast blade flashing, the organs rejected seconds before the blood welled up.

Sugarbag flies were everywhere around the horses. When Old Bill started to move with his caravan, it was at a slow, leisurely pace so the flies had no difficulty in keeping up and adding to his and the old horses' misery.

While Gene Autry, Roy Rogers, Hopalong Cassidy and their like dealt with the problem of the day with smoking guns, a fast flamboyant horse and a tuned guitar, Old Bill possessed none of these. He had only a boiling tar pot and his whip.

He always seemed to have to make a detour to the Six Mile Pub to check the service line. After drinking his share and collecting a shout for the track from Jack (Bushie) Woodland, he would commence the final leg of day one on the pipeline track. The old horses were prone to habit, poley saddles were made well and the steed's back was broad. Bill Hurst would sleep on this journey, gently lolling in the saddle, the effects of Captain Kettle's finest wearing heavy. Halfway between Flapper's Hill and Sing's Garden on the King River track near the pipeline the animals would draw abreast at the long water trough. That was the end of the journey for the day.

First Camp

After a great effort, Bill would drop the saddle and set the animals to graze. No hobbles were needed. With his swag away from the water trough and night activity, he'd get a fire going and finally do justice to the package of food prepared by Alice Nixon from the meatworks' canteen. Again a sip from the stained quart pot, a religious draw on the pipe he held in one hand, and he would gaze longingly at the single, bright light at the front of the pub a few short miles across the salt marsh.

'Bloody Ringer Gibson,' he'd mutter to himself. 'That lanky bastard! Bet he's pissed to the eyebrows now. He was looking for a fight when I was leaving. Reckon that half-breed Maori from Queensland, Dave Malloy, would have flogged the shit out of him by now. Ugly bastard! Big and nuggety. They say he can king-hit like the kick of a mule. Would like to see him have a go with that young fella Don MacLachlan. Came in with a mob of bullocks the other day. Mob from the Territory. Big young fella, good arms and shoulders. Must have been working hard since he was a kid. Can't remember if he smoked at all. Good lookin' larrikin. Old man must have been a returned soldier and a horseman. What about that young yella fella from Spring Creek? Same build, but shorter, husky voice. July Oakes, that's his name. Never gave up, they say. Took on both the MacMicking brothers, both bigger Kimberley men. A battle to remember. He and Teddy Farghurson had a real stoush at the Wyndham Picture Gardens behind Joe Mosey's shop this season. Shit! I missed that one. Wason Byers, from the Territory, giant of a man, would have flogged the lot, unless you had a .303 to break even! God bless Ireland!'

Bill's mind settled on more pleasant thoughts as the embers cooled. 'Stuff the *Koolinda* this year. Not going south. The last bloody trip down the coast nearly ruined my drinkin'. Bloody sea-sickness! And that early bloody wet weather off Onslow, too close to that cyclone. Old Captain Jardine can get nicked! Anyway his scotch is up to shit! He can save it for those Derby nurses and that governess from Fitzroy somewhere. Wish I was younger.'

The dingoes were coming off the stony hills now and preparing for the hunt. The curlews would come in much later; their morbid cries would continue until piccaninny dawn. None of the bush and night activity troubled Bill Hurst. He had removed his old hat long ago. The night air was cool and gently he ruffled his greying temple. Lying in his swag, easy now, face aglow with the effect of the overproof rum, he gazed at his bottle and grunted when the level of the contents registered. 'Might have to crack another before we draw the rein at the King tomorrow. Can't have those buggers out there helpin' me with my grog supply. They won't hit town till Friday.'

For safety, stockmen slept with their trousers on and the need for a second belt was obvious. Bill's other belt—with the pocket watch, waxed matchbox and the old timer pocketknife, all in soft leather pouches—lay conveniently near his pillow. 'Bloody braces!' Bill would curse. 'Anyway, need to keep me strides on. Somehow.'

Nearby lay the .44 colt with the wooden grip handle. Old Bill was most reluctant to discharge a round to frighten off the wild dogs. The horses would only be spooked if the dingoes came near, but if they took fright they would not run away but form their own defence and lash out with their hind hooves. They would always be back there the next day; Bill's little bag containing molasses and quality grain guaranteed that.

As usual, Scully Johns, a butcher in the meatworks, had already asked him if he was staying for the wet after the season. His answer was yes, and he would again care for his shed and dwelling on the Wyndham foreshore next door to Bill Flinders' garage. It was cheap living between seasons. The pub was across the road; Gee Hong Yet's general store and Mrs Flinders' drapery were around the corner. Everything he required was a short stroll away, except the bloody post office. It would have to be on the other end of the one-horse town.

Most importantly, Bill could live within the confines of the so-called English gentry, the aristocrats, a breed apart that guaranteed him connections in the community that in turn guaranteed his protection. He belonged with the Caucasian section that defied the elements, broke the code of the Kimberley hinterland and set about producing a stark, new culture. There were unwritten, clearly understood rules which reinforced the continuity and symbolism of the existence of the British Empire. Like others, Bill did not fraternise with so-called bludgers, blacks, foreigners or any others who had no association with the Anglo–Australian culture. You could not be called a 'gin jockey' unless you actually disgraced yourself and sired a yellow bastard. 'Thank the Lord it didn't happen to me,' Bill thought. 'Come to think of it, I didn't go lookin'. Should have, maybe. I don't know. No guts!'

Bill thought about the local identities as he lay beside the fire. 'There were some half-castes, like Edgar and Cyprian Birch, Wilfred Pierce and Ernie Chapman. Talk to them in the street, but that's about all. There were Paddy and Ida, black people who worked for Bill Flinders. Servants, who did every task there was, domestic help. Doug Davidson, now there was a man, him and his young air hostess wife. Flamboyant pin-stripe moustache, pith hat, Kimberley creams, long khaki socks and shining brown shoes. Think he's just got off the state ship *Koolinda* from bloody London! Got money too. Anyway, all in the breeding. They say he never had blacks to help him in the house. Paid his hired help, he did. Principle out of place. Him and them bloody Chinamen! Thank God there's only three families left in town. They do all the work themselves, use their kids. Poor bloody kids. All work, no play. What a way to make a quid! Could have fooled me!

'And that Scully Johns was a cunning mongrel. Worked all the season cutting up beef into quarters and chimes*, then finished up at the end of August. Went bush catching bloody finches and making an extra quid. Always wondered why he shipped up the 4x4 Chevy Blitz truck. Worse still, the bloody blackfellas on Carlton Station made him rich. Just for a few sticks of nicky nicky. Apparently he would deliver a truckload of cages and bird catching equipment to his manager friends on various cattle stations. They'd then organise station Aboriginals to catch the prized finches at least a month or so prior to the opening of the official finch-trapping season. Old Scully would have the advantage in numbers and varieties caught and that would affect his sales and prices. Other trappers lost out miserably when, having searched the known locations out bush, they found out that the birds had been whisked away before the season began. He will die rich, they tell me.

'No wonder that cunning little crooked-arm jockey, Flusher Larkin, is trying to get a bird trapping licence. Bloody womaniser. Half his luck, the bastard! Scraven Tord, the humped-back old shit. He's got a licence now. Stuffed without the blackfellas. Caught out

---

*The front and hind legs of a beast

cattle duffing on Moonlight Valley, gotta prove he's a white man somehow. Joe Somerfield from Cow Creek Station's helping him out. Pity Doug Davidson doesn't know about the extra quid he's makin' on his time. What's them old blackfellas helping him? Demon and Slippery, that's them, they know the country. Can't trust that old Paddy Carol, he's a Davidson man. Dob them in! Reminds me, I haven't seen my drinkin' mate, Gene French, for a while. He'll show up at the Six Mile Pub soon enough after contracting another windmill on the route. As a worker he's not as good as Norman Osmond, but then he can't bloody possibly be with his stiff hand and fingers. Besides, he's too bloody big.'

The night was quiet, only the gentle wind blew, the ash on the yellow jack bush timber coals was glowing. Old Bill had again forgotten to place the screw-top lid on the coffee and chicory jar. The Southern Cross was there in all its splendour. The dingoes were unusually quiet for a little while. They knew! So did the two old horses. Their nostrils flared, their withers quivering, the full length of their flanks shaking. The strong taint in the air lingered as the remnants of the King River's Indigenous people silently passed by, protected by the darkness. Old Bill was still awake, but saw nothing, heard nothing, smelt nothing. But they saw him many times. Tonight they would stop their walk at Flapper's Hill (Boola-Njee) camp, and leave for the cover of the mangroves at dawn. Big tide the next day, fish to be caught!

Daybreak, following the pipeline in the sandy areas before the King River, there were no expected dramas or massive water leakages. Old Bill had passed the salt troughs and spring, the usual Afghan camp and the last cattle camp on the Karunjie stock route. This was Sik Anna's camp where he rested his camels prior to his journey with domestic loads or delivering cattle. Only a few short years earlier this practice had stopped.

A road had now been built to Karunjie and Gibb River stations, allowing four-wheel drive trucks to pass through, but only in the dry season. In the 1940s, directly after World War II, there was a surplus of second-hand trucks left at Wyndham and Truscott army bases by the departing American and Australian armed forces. Bill had also passed close by Sing's Garden. The ruins would be still visible in years to come, the remains of the well, house and garden area evidence of the exploits of the common Chinese market gardener in and around Wyndham.

Stockmen

With the help of camels and mules, the pastoralists had finally succeeded in constructing a wheel track for a four-wheel drive truck. Now with the luxury of the road and a truck supplied by station owners to carry equipment, the business of moving store cattle from the station to the meatworks had become more convenient. The Karunjie Station truck was now parked off the track over two hundred yards from the first cutting on the hill. Bill could not progress any further. 'Bloody bullocks! Hope they don't shift that loose pipe in the guts of the cutting.'

His eyes took in the scene. 'Shit! Another bottle of rum sacrificed. Bloody Dave Rust! Scottie bloody Salmon. They're a couple of days early, trying to pick up a bit of fat at Chimoolie. A lot of good that's going to do, though. Frank Pober, the meat-works' head stockman, will dob them in to old man Ferguson.'

Still seated in front of the truck was the driver, Jack Campbell, a big part-Aboriginal Queenslander. A stockman, he had worked his way across the Top End with another adventurous cattleman called Jack Green, who had his own droving plant and was also working from around the Halls Creek area.

Jack Campbell eased his massive body out of the old Blitz truck.

He took off his dusty hat, stretched and prepared to meet the 'pipeline cowboy'. Jack was not a religious man but he muttered a word of thanks to the Almighty for the welcome sight moving towards him on the ancient horse. 'There's a nip in those bags,' Bill said.

'Me bloody aching bones,' Jack sighed as he stretched again.

Jack had suffered a great deal as a result of an accident. Whilst mustering on the plains of a Queensland cattle station, alone, apart from the mob and pursuing wild unbranded cattle, his horse stumbled and fell, throwing him off. He sustained a clean break to one leg and before he could grab the flying reins, the frightened horse quickly bunched itself together and bolted towards the distant mass of cattle in the main herd. No one had seen the mishap or noticed the lathering, riderless horse dragging its reins limping through the light scrub and plains country.

Jack Campbell was no fool. While still in a state of shock, he had braced his leg with bush wood and secured it with his shirt and his other belt. The weather was cool so he would need his coat and would only cut it up if necessary. It was some miles to the camp. Maybe some of the crew would notice his absence or, if they saw his horse return to the camp, they might come in search of the rider. But no one would be overly concerned. In those days, men often made decisions to watch a good group of wild fat cattle alone, all night by themselves, up a dry gully with a fire at the entrance. Sometimes too, men deserted the mustering camp for a night's ride back to the homestead if it was near. Or they'd go for a little bit of black velvet, turn up back at the camp at daylight. To the usual queries of their whereabouts they would shamelessly respond: 'I got lost a bit in the scrub. Me horse got knocked up. I was forced to have a dry camp!'

Jack was made of better stuff, however. He waited until sundown, nearly exhausted his tobacco supply, and sat beside the fire he had lit. Occasionally he threw on a green branch so as to create smoke. Painfully reserving his strength he searched the horizon in the direction of the camp. No one came. Only the hawks, the carrion from above and one black crow found him sitting rejected and physically vulnerable. Soon the dingoes would scent the smoke and, with their ground-covering, fast, loping pace, eventually they would show up.

Jack knew this, and after sundown decided to drag himself away from the smoke backwards to the camp. He had confidence in his huge muscular arms, and his boots were new and would take a lot of wear. Gabardine trousers were always tough. The burning pain in his leg gave him the determination to get on with the job ahead. He placed his wax matches and pocketknife in his coat pockets at the ready. After all, this was dingo country, and should they loom out of the darkness he would quickly throw a light into the large clumps of spinifex grass that dotted the stony plain.

His arduous journey began. Two hundred yards along the way, he selected a strong piece of wood to serve as a club, should the dingoes follow up the blood-scented trail. With his new weapon tucked through his trouser belt, Jack steeled himself for a journey that would take all night and part of the next day.

Being a man of few words, after reluctantly serving a term in a distant Queensland hospital, Jack returned to the station merely to collect his pay. This was no station for a yella fella, no one cared and you were always expendable. Aargh well!

The Boss Boy

Two middle-aged, full-blood Aboriginal women sat on the truck among the piles of droving equipment and swags. Their huge floppy hats almost covered their faces as they patiently gazed back at the gathering, billowing dust, now just around the low hill. Bullocks were close up; they could hear the cut horns clashing as they were forced through the wheel-track width between the sheer cut hill and the thirty-five pound railway line fence, the only protection from falling into the King River. The tide was out, revealing treacherous muddy slopes, angling downwards at forty-five degrees and in some places, a sheer drop of about thirty feet from track to the water's surface.

It would be a traumatic time for the stockman leading, out front of the bullocks. The lead bullocks would become fidgety from being jostled and pushed from behind. Moving into unknown territory and now smelling saltwater for the first time, they would be nervously wanting to pause and look ahead towards the unfamiliar figure on the horse, showing the direction.

The boss boy, always an Aboriginal recognised for his leadership, somehow ended up with this dangerous job. Treacherous to say the least. Usually he would be on the wing and behind the herd a little, but unconcerned, casually moving with the herd, glad there were only four more camps left. 'Whitefellas,' he would think. 'Shit scared of bullock, might be they push him off the edge into the mud. Might be crocodile grab him, more smaller than bullock. Might be horse chuck him underneath bullock. Might be I all right.'

He deliberately rode further in front than usual, allowing himself time and space should anything go wrong. All of his reflexes were on full alert. 'I know,' he thought. 'Boss gonna give me this job. I been save this old creamy mare for today. She been with me last year, she know. Anyway!' His mind raced for reassurance. 'Old man Dave Rust, him all right, he look after us mob blackfellas from Karunjie. Good poor bugger.'

Cyprian and Polly Birch and children returning to Wyndham, 1943
artwork by Reg Birch

Shit cart run—Cyprian and Reg
artwork by Reg Birch

Forrest River Mission - married quarters, early 1920s

Unloading stores at Forrest River Mission

Afghans loading camel at Wyndham

Wyndham meatworks, with the Bastion Ranges, and the jetty in foreground

Wyndham panorama, taken from the crow's nest of a visiting ship, c.1920s

Ah Kim's market garden, Parry's Creek

The grandstand, Wyndham race meeting, during the era when Reg's parents came to town

Pupils from Wyndham Primary
School c.1947

LtoR: Ann Ferguson,
Mrs Redding, Bob Casey,
Ron Patching, Jill Patching,
Pam De Vries, Rosemary Birch,
Trevor Wilhelm, Laurie Birch,
Reg Birch, George Patching,
Jennifer Ryle, unidentified,
Alan Kershaw, Ken Johnson,
Ray De Vries, Helen Birch,
unidentified.

Senior pupils from
Wyndham Primary School
c.1953

Back LtoR:
Frank Chulung,
Reg Birch,
Autry Andrews,
Steve Smith.
Front LtoR:
John Auburn, Tom Birch,
Kim Woodland,
Ian Mansfield,
Paul Whittaker (obscured)
Ted Birch.

Helen, Ted, Reg and Len, outside our house in the Gully, Wyndham

Left: Reg Birch, 1955. Hunting with traditional people at Goose Hill Creek

Below: Reg Birch, 1953/54 boy scout troop leader, Wyndham 53rd group

Cyprian Burt and Polly Ogden's wedding, 4 July 1935
L to R: Frank B. Lacy, Cyprian, Polly, Ivy Mills, Eileen Edwards

Margaret and Reg's wedding, 1965

Dust

The dust-choked cattle kept on bellowing. There was no push from the drovers behind the herd. The cattle expected to follow the leader on the horse at their own pace; their instinct was to surge together. Dave Rust, pipe in mouth, sat astride his horse, watching. The ground was pounded to dust where over six hundred plus cattle had just passed. His saddle was still making ominous, creaking-leather noises. Guilty as hell, it was he who normally, as the boss drover, would lead the bullocks at all times. He had only mounted the horse after the King River camp near the prison tree. There was no need for him to ride a horse, when he could enjoy the luxury of the old, jolting four-wheel drive truck until they reached the extremes of Wyndham. Scottie Salmon would keep an eye on the blacks. Then again, he didn't have to. They were a good mob, expert with bullocks, gentle with horses. The boss boy was now getting on in years, but the younger Aboriginal fellas were always full of laughs and good humour. They loved this work, and a visit to Wyndham. A few more days and they would certainly wet the old whistle.

The dust died down, the south-east wind clearing it after the bottleneck. 'Don't know who I would put in that old man's place up front of the herd,' Dave thought. 'Thank God he is doing my job. Don't know who worries about me nowadays. Don't know if the family's still around in Scotland. Wouldn't have a clue. Who cares? Must return one day and check them out if ever I make a decent quid.'

The cattle broke into a casual canter when they sensed the freedom. Then, as the whole herd came free of the tight stock route, they slowed to a grazing pace. The drovers had also halted. The blackfellas knew their two masters, Dave Rust and Scottie Salmon, had now spotted Bill Hurst having a yarn with Jack.

A stroke of luck, a sniff and a taste before delivery. God bless Scotland, stuff Ireland. An almost wordless direction to the boss boy to take the mob to the dinner camp. 'Watch the mob there, and don't forget to wing them two strangers, keep him outside. (This meant simply to keep the two bullocks with the Gibb River brand on the fringe of the herd, ready for selection and slaughter for their own consumption and payment for favours from friends in the township of Wyndham.) Old Bert Sharpe might be coming out this arvo. Look out for his Willy's Jeep (the American general purpose four-wheel drive vehicle). Take the bullocks slow now, old man.'

Old Bill spat on the ground. 'Lost me bloody supply!' he thought to himself. 'There's only one thing worse than a thirsty Scotsman. Two of the bastards! Have to give the big yella fella a nip once the blacks are out of sight, as well.'

Jack Campbell was familiar with the ritual. He had already sent the two women walking along the track, suggesting that they go walkabout looking for big fat goannas. Their hairy mongrel dog would help sniff out those now buried underground, fat and well into winter's hibernation. They also knew what was about to happen. Apart from the several canteens and the forty-four gallon drum of water on the truck, there were two calico water bags hanging off the side. Cunningly, his quart pot in hand, Jack positioned himself, blocking off all access, pretending to get a drink. His thirst for the liquid blessing was just as demanding as that of his white counterparts. They could not insult old Bill's obligatory shout and take the liquor straight. Water was the mediator in this stark Kimberley frontier.

'There's a nip for you mate!' Dave said to Jack. 'Bert is coming soon, perhaps a little later.'

They had to be careful. 'Can't be seen to be feeding these yella fellas grog. The Native Welfare will be onto ya like a ton of bricks.'

Dave had a white mate, now in gaol for supplying liquor to a native. 'That bloody copper, Des Sculthorp, could come out any-way, looking for free beef. He's a bad bastard, that one. Look at that mob he had in chains, a while back. Poor miserable bastards. Don't know what they done to deserve that. Nothing to say to him that day. Lot of howling down the station camp that night. Even the dogs joined in. King bloody George hasn't a clue what's happening in his kingdom!'

Dinner Camp

They stayed longer than intended. Dinner camp became night camp. No one had told the Aboriginal stockmen to go any further. Bullocks spread out over the plain, grazing greedily on the salt grasses. The women had walked into the camp at dinner-time with three fat goannas. The white men alone would eat salt beef, damper and onion that evening.

Mid-afternoon saw the arrival of the old Karunjie truck. Jack Campbell was still driving, but at an extremely sedate pace. First gear to be exact, with two boisterous Scotsmen on the pile of gear on the back, both vigorously debating whether John L. Sullivan or Gentleman Jim Corbett was superior in the art of fisticuffs as designated by the Marquis of Queensbury. The two tethered horses of the Kimberley's finest stockmen sauntered along behind. All three men would sleep under the truck tonight. It was new country for the bullocks—some sand, some black soil. Any hollow ground could spook them and cause them to rush.

There would be no watch tonight for the white men. The Aboriginal stockmen would double their watch anyway. Their reward would be passed over in silence after they got to town. An extra stick of tobacco or a red or blue shirt from old man Lee

Tong's shop. The balance was always there. Bert Sharpe did not come. An added blessing indeed.

Neither Scottie Salmon nor Dave Rust knew that the bush Aboriginal people from the King River tribe were always near. Old man Ngidil and his small group had actually walked behind the herd from Bindoola Creek above the Durack River. Every night they visited the Aboriginal stockmen who slept apart, then they feasted on station beef and damper to their hearts' content. The Aboriginal stockmen would dutifully supply all the materials needed by the people. Saddle cloths, leather strips, billycans, sugar and flour bags, horse shoes and nails, would somehow become dislodged only to be picked up by the following harvesters, almost invisible in the distant mirages on the marsh, unseen against the backdrop of the bush.

During the day the bush people would follow the tree line on the edge of marsh, out of sight. At Slatey Creek, the King River bush people parted company and took the shortcut through Mirranala (Diggers Rest), crossed the river over the rock bars at low tide early in the morning and gained two days in front of the walking bullocks on the stock route. With their booty safely stashed away from fire they would prepare to poison fish in the bomb holes in the saltwater creeks and share the catch with their kinsmen now working for survival at the Six Mile Pub. Oswald Johnson, Munjee, son of King Peter Warriu, would be glad to see them.

The white men moving through the bush rarely looked behind. They would never know what boab trees, creeks, large rocks and other standard landmarks looked like from the other side. This was the reason why they frequently became disoriented and eventually lost. Death, as they should have known, comes quickly for the foolhardy in the Kimberley.

The Pumping Station

Each morning Bill Hurst would slowly go through his ritual. He'd mount his horse and with the gained height, draw the reins to study the northern horizon. 'Yes,' he would acknowledge when he eventually saw the dust brought up by the slowly moving herd. 'Everything's all right. What would we do without blackfellas?'

His daily journey began all over again. Hours later, he would have to drop his swag again for a dinnertime camp. 'Somewhere away from the bloody mosquitoes,' he wished.

As Bill plodded slowly along the foothills on the powdered dust, he marveled at what appeared before him mile after mile. Countless insects, reptiles and small animals which dared to expose themselves in the newly-created open and dangerous space on the stock route were gobbled up by larger birds and animals. Dingoes and crows understood quickly. Like Aboriginal people, they followed the herds until they reached the boundaries of their territory. Eagles, kestrels, kookaburras and other birds of prey made their spectacular kills amid clouds of exploding dust. The carrion waited. Tiny snakes and small lizards committed suicide. They found no traction in their panic and floundered, flustered in their haste to cover the open stretch of ground that had not existed there the day before. A larger snake had no difficulty crossing the stock route slowly, but if it was attacked by a large eagle or kookaburra, it would not be able to speed up in the loose dust and reach the safety of the bush.

At last the tin shacks of the pumphouse quarters would come into view. 'No one will be there. All away doing something or another. Mid-afternoon. Too bloody hot now,' Old Bill would mutter.

The horses would be unpacked, washed down with pressured water from the tattered old rubber and canvas hose and then placed in the yard near the boab tree. There was always some good dry chaff or oats with a taste of molasses. 'Old Dobbin will love that. Oh yes! Got to put on the fly swishers, poor buggers.'

At last a thought for himself. 'A quick nip, throw the swag on the mattress on the cyclone bunk. Get some kip on the verandah. No flappers out here to have a gander at me balls, take me itching strides off. Have a shave tomorrow, had the shakes this morning. Would have cut me bloody throat if I tried! Can't be bothered getting the razor strop and blade out of me pouch anyway. Shit! Me foot's a bit on the bloody nose. Have a bogey later. Bloody flies. Now where did I put me menthoid tablets? Bloody kidneys.'

Long after Bill succumbed to sleep, Marty Vaughn came in quietly, late in the afternoon, and saw the old chap snoring his head off. Flat on his back, grey flannels stretched tightly over his enormous heaving belly and just like his old horses, one foot twitching spasmodically at the ever-present, moisture seeking flies. 'Old bastard's made it again. One day the horses will come in without him.'

He would pause only for a while, take a good look at the veins on Bill's hawk-like features, the grey hairs scraggly and protruding unchecked out of his huge nose. Several bloated, blood-filled mosquitoes, he noticed, squatted on the contours of Bill's aged face and arms.

'Better call it quits soon, old timer,' Marty said. 'If that old croc in the cutting don't get you, the sun and the booze will surely put paid to you. Heard tell they're gonna get one of those new fangled four-wheel drive jeeps to do your job. Right hand drive too! Not one of those Yank tin boxes. Know where you'd end up, you old bugger! Hope you make it for the *Koojarra* or *Kabarli*, whichever's your ticket south.

'That bloody engineer Kershaw, too smart for his britches, won't let sleeping dogs lie. Might be the last mob of cattle to pass through here they reckon. Old man Wally Ferguson dropped the rumour, another meatworks out of Glenroy Station or somewhere out that way. Save the cattle from the walk in, losin' fat and all that. Gonna fly them in on aeroplanes. What bloody next?' Marty tried to clear his memory. 'That young fella Emile Barclay, works on the killing floor there somewhere, he told me they're gonna use Bristol freighters, bigger aeroplanes than the old DC3, with doors that open up in the front of the plane. Never heard of it before. What bloody next?'

Delivery Camp

The horse tailer was already at Chimoolie. By mid-afternoon, Jack Campbell was also there with the complete camp and gear. The herd was grazing towards the dam. Already the lead bullocks could smell the fresh water across the plain. The afternoon sea breeze from the Cambridge Gulf was strong and picking up. As Dave Rust rested with his swag against a gutta-percha tree, writing in his stockman's log, he thought of old Bert Sharpe. 'He's late, the bastard,' he grumbled loudly. 'Promised me a drop in return for the clean skin killer. Guess he'll come good. The beef's not mine and any grog he's got, he's snaffled from the station loading. Vicious bloody circle! Old bugger. Tom Quilty can go beggin'. The rich bastard!'

Dave's eyes took in the distant saddle in the mountain range south of their camp. 'Those bloody Afghans—got to hand it to them,' he thought. 'Built a camel track over that stony hill to the Six Mile Pub. Anything to save a day's walk. Bit steep for my liking. Anyway, not going lead my horse over on foot.'

Before the sun dipped behind the Erskine Range, a vehicle approached from the south. It followed the usual track and then, as it approached the cattle, respectfully went bush and gave them a wide berth. 'Yes,' Dave thought. 'It's Bert's jeep all right, but not him driving.'

Don Sharpe, still a boy, drove the jeep, unknowingly bringing clouds of red dust into the stock camp. 'Yeah, we could do with some more dust,' Jack Campbell muttered. 'Good on ya, lad!'

Dave neither saw nor felt the dust. His appetite had already been brought on by Bill Hurst's meagre offering two days before at the King River. There could have been a blue between Jack and Scottie. It would have been a one-sided event, with the difference in size between those two. Gotta think twice about bringin' bloody women along next time. Bloody little rooster, that Scottie Salmon, all guts and balls, no friggin' brains. Arrh well.'

He focused on the disciple from Wyndham. The Willys' four-wheel drive jeep came to a halt.

'Gidday.'

No one said anything else. With skill, Bert unfolded his massive body from the dust-covered vehicle. He was past middle-age but his shoulders, arms and hands told you what he did for a living. The son, a stripling but already an image of the old man, came around from the other side of the jeep.

'My gut tells me someone's cut me bloody throat!' Dave Russ exclaimed as he rose and shook the firm hand, confirming that he had kept his bargain.

The killer, a bullock selected along the stock route for the purposes of meat supply or bargaining power, was not really a clean skin. It was castrated, and had its horns cut. It flashed a Gibb River brand, and was already separated in a small herd of fifteen other beasts held off by a young Aboriginal stockman near a clump of trees. They had been waiting for almost an hour; such was the thirst of the drovers. After greetings all around, Bert reached into the back of the jeep. He had previously cut a forty-four gallon drum in half from top to bottom. One portion now lay on its side in the back and held a full block of ice purchased from Jack Woodland at the pub. The negotiated price was a rump and a salted brisket. No sense in him asking for chuck steak! On top were two gallons of bottled beer still in their straw jackets and two bottles of rum wrapped in a light hessian bag, more for their protection than for keeping them cold. Leaving the rum till later, he brought out three bottles of beer. 'You got your quart pots? Here! Wash down the dust.'

Young Don settled down for a long wait. He would miss the pictures tonight. Too late, as always, he would realise the cunning of his father. His mother Polly would be home with his sister Ethel; they were older and knew what to expect when old timers met.

Scottie Salmon had also noticed the arrival of the jeep. As usual he passed on the responsibility of his early evening watch of the herd of cattle to the boss boy. He knew that Bert Sharpe would have a cold beer with his brand on it. All he had to do was to fulfil his part of the bargain.

On a given signal, Scottie Salmon, on his third refill, climbed the tree and prepared the old .303 Enfield rifle. On the first pass through with the group of beasts, he neatly shot the chosen bullock between the eyes. It dropped to the ground. With his Green River brand butcher's knife, Scottie then cut its throat and skillfully bled it dry. After wiping the blade on the grass, he walked back to the stock camp and grog supply. The Aboriginal stockmen, experts in the trade, would skin and portion the beef cuts and place them on leaves in the upright forty-four gallon drum on the back of the jeep.

Young Don sat on the jeep and watched.

That night the cattle rushed. The drumming sound of hooves was deafening, frightening. One of the Aboriginal stockmen was dragged by the stirrup while trying to mount a panic-stricken horse. He survived with bruised ribs and severely lacerated arms. He also lost one boot. He'd track it down tomorrow; it would be there, unless the dingoes got it. Tomorrow was delivery day for the cattle. Frank Pober would check the count and then ride through to the meatworks with the bullocks.

Poor Fellas

'Poor fellas!' the Aboriginal stockmen would say. 'We been walk him long way. All the way from country (Karunjie). He singin' out now. He know, new saltwater country. He can smell already. Bullock been die here. Too many, poor bugger!'

They also had news to pass on to the Wyndham town blackfellas as well as Forrest River Mission people. The tribe would be ready after bullock season; walkabout time was almost upon them. Throw away the boots and brimmed hat, hide the new red shirt and green gabardine trousers. Their minds would be overflowing with the anticipation of reliving the experiences of the last wet—Aboriginal business and the annual visit to their own birthplace, the land which owned them.

The powerful horse and leather odours were only faint now. The old man, the boss boy, now in his usual position riding the outside wing of the stretched herd, stood up in the stirrups and watched the meatworks' head stockman count the bullocks through the double gates. He could see the saltwater country already, mangrove leaves turning salty side up with the south-east winds blowing. Countless tiny green and grey mangrove birds chattered away, happily singing their territorial anthems.

'Bloody sandflies!' the old man thought. His work was almost over, only the return journey with the horses was left. 'Horse tailer and them boasting young fellas can do that!'

He was another with the responsibility of passing on important information. After the boss gave them their pay, he would talk to old man Hector (Jarlngah) who worked for Billy Flinders. Jarlngah, tall, dignified, with traditional initiation body scars, ever silent, a pillar, and the communications link in old Wyndham town. Jimmy and Ida (Binji-Binji and Jundingalli) were not of this traditional tribal area but remained as stalwarts in the area nonetheless. He'd talk to them too. The Karunjie Station cattle were on the marsh near Parry's Creek. The boss boy's body succumbed to the saddle, eyes in a glaze, his mind already immersed in the Kimberley hinterland, spirit country. 'This time would be different,' he thought. 'There was mourning to deal with. The bones of that great uncle were ready.'

Everybody who was somehow connected to the family had the serious obligation to be at the chosen time and place. The droving season and whitefella's loading trucks served to improve the bush telegraph. But as the time drew near, his people reverted to traditional methods. Smoke signals would advise the advance parties who were traveling constantly, day and night.

Selected bones and hair of the deceased would be wrapped in paperbark and symbolically daubed in red and white ochre. As the distant smoke of advancing tribes blew across the Cambridge Gulf and small gatherings drew closer together, the tension mounted. Women would cut their hair, a sign of mourning and a sacrifice of their dignity. There was much wailing and crying; they would strike their bare heads with hand-sized stones, inflicting gaping, bleeding wounds, openly displaying their pain. There would be some scores to settle when all concerned finally met. A middle-aged man wearing only a hair belt, eyes wide and unblinking, body erect and taut, would step aside, already prepared with his battle regalia. His single bladed spear at the ready, horizontal in his left hand, with the other hand deliberately rattling the throwing stick and chosen spear.

The others would know. This was not a challenge. It was a defence with honour, should anyone think otherwise. There could be blood and more mourning, but it was the Law. Skillfully the old men would take control and speak rapidly to bring about a settling of angered minds. The mock taunts and gestures would turn to signs of acceptance. This would not happen every time. Sometimes there would be a serious clash and someone would get hurt.

Perhaps the family had not been dutiful and had not protected the deceased person. Why did it happen? Was his death punishment for a misdemeanor in his younger days? Was it his right to kill his young second wife? He had to do it, only way to stop them young bucks from that saltwater country.

'Them young yella fellas from the mission, they cunning,' he thought. 'Steal horses and pack and rifle. Go anywhere with young lubra*, they like them too. Runaway. Shovel spear can't catch him up sometime. Smart bastards, some of them! They tell missionary and policeman he only looking for dog and eagle-hawk. Get money from Roads Board in Wyndham. He biggest bullshit, too. How many time they shoot our camp dogs and steal our young girls? Nearly bad as the whitefella. Them mob not from this country, nobody know him, might be one day, he lose himself longa swag or longa bush. Blackfella might be catch him up longa shovel spear. That gin too! Teach him proper way. Yella fella bastard! That Welfare bloke been come quick fella when that yella fella kid been born down the creek. Them two old women been givem that young lubra biggest belting, make him (the young woman concerned) sit up and listen and bleed, close up, nearly finish him (kill her). Nearly kill that kid too, skin not from us, I don't know. Whiteman bastard!'

---

*A derogatory term for an Aboriginal woman

As the herd of cattle rounded the Bastion Range the old man's thoughts rambled on. The meatworks with its towering smoke stack came into view. Close up now.

'Some good half-caste in town. Old man Cyprian Birch, buggered-up leg, tough old bastard. Big family, got no country! See him tomorrow. He Bunuba, Jack tell me, got relation working at Mount House Station, big mob there. He got a gramophone too. I reckon we can play them old Tex Morton and Buddy William record. Might be he sing and play his old squeezebox. Might be we get drunk. Look out! Wuddai! Might be better, we fellas sit down quiet. Policeman lock him up us mob. Like them other mob, poor fellas, early days, policeman been steal him, take him 'way. Never been come back to country. Poor bugger!'

The smoke from Wulmah, just across the Gulf, told him the tribe had already started the journey. It meant that they were weeks into their journey from across the Forrest River and now moving over the hills towards Nulla Nulla outstation at the southern end of the Aboriginal reserve. 'The policeman never went that way.'

They would never cross or swim saltwater rivers, because of the hazard of crocodiles in the mangrove swamps and soft dark deep mud. Horses would panic in this environment so trackers always took them the long way around. 'Them blackfella trackers them frightened bugger too. Blackfellas from other country, I don't know, sometime they relation, sometime they not. They reckon they sing him by and by! They bad bugger, nobody cry for them!'

Then his thoughts led him to another story, 'Might be only them two girl from that 'nother country, other side river all right, two fella all the same, twin they call him. Blackfella Law say one gotta die. Good job, Mummy been runaway early time, take him two fella bush, close up Wyndham to Ah Kim's shop. He got sister there living with that old Chinaman. Might be they kill him

129

proper, them two fella piccaninny if they never shift camp. Two fella got yella fella piccaninny now anyway. This country watch him, Warriu! Good enough! Yo.'

The sharp crack of Dave Rust's whip brought the old boss boy back from his thoughts. The heat was rising and the agitated cattle were realising they were again being forced into a bottle-neck. The end of the road. The old man had almost forgotten the plight of the bullocks. It would leave his mind for another year.

The Meatworks

Wally Ferguson had deliberately placed his government-owned '49 Ford Mercury a long way from the approaching cattle and the incoming dust. Its immaculate, glistening body with white hubs on the large wheels, was a symbol of the existing colonial bureaucracy: the manager's car, a mark of the gentry. It confirmed Wally's undisputed ranking. In status he was equalled only by the visiting magistrate and police inspector.

He now stood a good fifty yards away, safely behind the extended steel wing that led into the holding yards. The cattle could smell the water in the troughs and the leaders broke in to a lazy trot. About two thousand white cockatoos simultaneously took to the wing. Agitated by the intrusion, they circled, aided by the south-east wind, looking like a huge white lace curtain gently blowing in the breeze—in spite of those little dry squawking throats and white bird droppings raining down!

'Thank God they leave at sundown every day to go and sleep in the bush,' Wally thought. 'Don't know why the missus wants to keep one in a cage!'

His thoughts were cut short. True to form, Wally's professional self took over. 'The bullocks don't look too bad, considering.'

Dave Rust approached out of the dust, the fall of his whip dragging on the ground between the fore and hind legs of his magnificent looking chestnut horse. The old gooseneck pipe upside down in his mouth, he drew rein, dismounted and coughed a long, rasping, gurgling cough. 'Shit!'

Wally Ferguson looked at the clean-shaven drover. He did not greet every delivering drover, but here was a kindred spirit, a man with connections to the old country, Scotland. It wasn't necessary to mention the Coat of Arms or an attachment to various counties or manors, there was just an instinctive recognition of each other through the brogue. Enough bastards hiding under the hat and spur to found another colony, there were. Bet my first shilling there's an Irishman on the route as well, but a bloke wouldn't know until pay day at the pub. Cocky bastards.

'Good day to you, old timer,' Wally welcomed Dave as he dismounted.

Dave Rust returned the handshake. 'Gidday!'

He gazed at this tall, big-boned man who had hundreds under his management. The white Panama hat shaded his craggy features, unkempt eyebrows carrying the shadow even further over his huge, red nose. A prominent feature among the Caucasian races, it seemed, reminiscent of the ragged mountain ranges in the background.

Wally's shirt was white with long sleeves and he sported a cravat to boot, further protection from the extreme Wyndham heat and dust that he would experience during his many excursions through his domain. The long, immaculately creased cream trousers flapped in the breeze, revealing the sheen of his brown shoes. The bone cigarette holder was still clenched between his aged, protruding yellow teeth.

The contrast between the two men was astounding. Of a similar age, both were in the same business but each had a different role and dressed accordingly.

Nothing much had to be said nor reported. The cattle delivery was now complete. The topic quickly changed.

'Who's going to win the Wyndham Cup this year? Joe Mosey got a chance, do you reckon?' Dave asked. 'Already heard from Bert that Hector Fuller's got some grain fed hack he's keeping quiet about,' he went on. 'He also tells me he's taken half a truck-load of chaff and grain down to Springvale. Bloody Quiltys and their secret imports from over east.'

'Depends,' Wally replied. 'There is going to be a big blue between these town jockeys, Joe Moore and Harold Caphorn and those bushies Mark Richards, sly old goat, and that stumpy half-caste, Sandy Harris. Can't trust them you know! Anyway, the races will see us wind up for the year. Give the ladies a chance to promenade.'

Dave had by now stoked his pipe and was almost at full steam. 'Do you want to see the first few through into the slaughter floor?' Wally asked. 'Big Archie's in fine form as usual, one beast per blow with his hammer. They wouldn't know what struck them.'

Both men moved towards the ramp that took the cattle up towards their final bellow. All the workmen noticed the boss and polished up a whisker. There were store cattle left over from the day before and everyone was flat strap, engrossed in their specialist task. The butchers were moving in controlled move-ments. Blood splattered their blades and aprons as each beast was effortlessly shredded of its wet hide and bled before beginning its journey around the floor on the shining steel hooks. A call came from a bloke at the gate on the enclosure with sprinklers. 'That's it, mate. Last of the bleeders from Ruby Plains.'

The noise was deafening as the frontrunners of the Karunjie mob now filled the slippery space. Horns and hooves clashed as bodies slammed against worn wooden palings. The catwalk on either side was a hive of activity with sweating, cursing, bellowing men. Long armed, battery-operated cattle prods were jabbed on the quivering rumps, causing some beasts to fall as their hind legs buckled under with the shock.

'Giddup bullock! Don't fall down here, get busted up, you only end up crow bait.' Each man had his own special language to talk to the beasts.

Dave Rust recognised the lead bullocks on the walk in from the holding paddock on Karunjie, the cattle station owned and managed by the government, although everything was coordinated by the administration of the Wyndham Meatworks. These cattle were the first to go here. Poor buggers. It was only a drover's thought.

'Well come on then,' the manager spoke first. 'There's no use hanging around here. Old man Patching will be waiting at the office with your cheque and loose pounds for the boys. Could also score a mug of tea if we are lucky.'

Wally Ferguson went through the ritual. 'When Jack Campbell brings the old truck in tomorrow for the usual repair job, tell him to drop in next door at the blacksmith's shop. Got those horseshoes and the new branding iron ready. Oh yes, the other thing, Crawshaw, the cooper, has got that half wooden vat stashed away for you. It's new wood, but he's had fat in it already and I think it will be just the ticket for curing your salt and corned beef.' He paused a few seconds and went on. 'Crawshaw's a quiet chap, doesn't go to the pub. I think he's a wardrobe drinker myself. It might be in your best interest to shout him a tot. Jack will have a snort behind the seat by then, I reckon.'

Casually he went through the list of duties he would be glad to arrange for his bushman friend. 'When we finish at the office, we'll drop in at the canteen and have a yarn with Joe Novell and get some decent bread for you.'

Wally was proud of his chief of staff's culinary skills but Dave merely nodded. 'Who wants to talk to that old fat so and so?' he thought to himself. Instead, he reminisced about last season's droving and the race meeting booze-up. Hopefully Alice Nixon would be here again this year. 'Now there's a woman who's got what it takes. Heart of gold, can handle any situation, could flog a pissed ringer with his hat, no worries. A bloody good woman she is! Pity that engine driver, Tommy Cross is sniffing around. Got a quid or two. Half his luck. Got to watch his mate on the other shift too. Ugly bastard don't like to talk to them blokes who stutter and mutter too much. Fight like a thrashing machine they tell me, old Roy O'Sullivan.'

Ferguson interrupted his thoughts. 'If you've got your general hardware list on you, we can give it to Dudley Morrison at the store. The Major will need two days to get it together anyway.'

Old Dave hated to be reminded of his responsibility, but old man Fergie was hurrying him along. Maybe he could sense his slight agitation. 'Yeah,' he answered.

They left the meatworks' office, crossed the railway lines and started onto the concrete ramp. On the way they chatted with the blacksmiths, barrel makers, hide stackers, engine drivers, and cold storage workers as well as old Bob MacLannen, who was on his way to the store for his morning tea.

On the Slate

The time had come for Dave's appointment with the Silver Fox. 'The waterhole's not opened yet but there's no harm in getting to the pub early.'

His memory excited his tastebuds, but a sense of duty reminded him that the drover's camp at the Nine Mile would already be set up. Jack and Scottie would now be waiting for the delivery mob to arrive, then unsaddle and hobble the remaining horses. They would have saved money for this occasion.

While Jack Campbell and the horse tailer were gathering wood for the camp, they noticed Bill Flinders' four-ton International truck on the salt marsh. 'Our timing's perfect as usual,' Jack thought. Race time. Again they've got all the blackfella prisoners cutting branches for the racecourse stables and stalls.'

There was only Paddy Flinders, an Aboriginal fella who had inherited his Caucasian boss's surname, driving the truck with one police boy watching the eight Aboriginal inmates. No one had concerns of prisoners bolting. This was a picnic for them. Paddy would make sure that they visited the clumps of trees near the station camps as they appeared daily in the preparations for the annual Wyndham Race meeting. There would be happy reunions, gentle embraces and soft, meaningful crying. Sometimes no words at all, only contact with tearful eyes. Everyone accepting the stories that had to be told.

'Hurry up, you mob!' Jack called out to his now excited crew.

The women had already unpacked the new salt beef prepared at Chimoolie. It was all placed on a steel cyclone bunk carried for this purpose and now covered with leaves for protection. In spite of all the precautions, someone had to stay and keep an eye on the camp and hunt away the usual stray camp dogs, as well as the hawks and crows and possible intruders. Scottie Salmon gave himself this task. It was no big deal.

Jack Whitten, the local taxi driver, had already delivered his first bottle of Bundaberg rum and a new packet of dark Havelock tobacco to Scottie Salmon, who smiled to himself upon receiving the ultimate luxury. 'On the slate,' he smiled to himself. 'My bloody name's still good. Pity that limpy-legged bugger delivered the stuff himself. Preferred the red haired wife. Didn't want her driving the new Humber Snipe taxi off the road, was his excuse. My arse! Sounds like bullshit to me.' There was a pause as reality struck. 'Can't argue though. Big bastard!'

He would fork out when the boss came good with his pay cheque, keep the peace. He had no desire to talk to anyone just yet. 'Have to drag my swag away from the camp before they all get back tonight,' he reminded himself. 'Hide a lump of that good salt beef for later. Drunken bastards. Jack Campbell's the worst. Can't shut him up, sing all bloody night. Won't sing around the bullocks, the big Queenslander bastard. Good night bloody Irene! Wish he'd learn another song. Anyway, who said he could sing? I'll have a go, if he throws shit at me.'

The rum was starting to take effect.

The Town Pub

Dave Rust got a ride into old Wyndham town. The younger driver, George Millard was not the best at all and continuously aggravated the interchange within the four-speed gearbox. It may not have been his fault. The vehicle he drove was a Ford one-ton utility, army surplus and had seen better days. 'Remind me not to give him a job,' Dave thought. 'He can't even double the bloody clutch.'

As he suspected, the pub was not open. 'No matter.' His mind searched for alternatives. 'I'll have a yarn with some of these blowflies sitting over at Freds' shop, better hide me hip flask though.'

He pretended to unclip his hip pocket watch and glanced at the sky. 'The sun passed the yard arm yet?'

Everyone grunted and turned to gaze at the closed door. They did not want to be reminded of the time. Dave took in the scene. His attempt at conversation was tinged with silent, mocking contempt. If Betty Grable walked past here strip bloody starkers, these old derelicts would not turn a hair. 'Gidday Frank,' he spoke politely now.

His real name was Frank Thomas, but locals called him Scrub Turkey. He was short and his body grotesque on account of a dislocated hip. With thick curly brown hair, horn-rimmed glasses and nicotine stained hands, he could only be described as a pen and paper pusher. A shiny bum. An office Johnnie.

There were other locals Dave also knew only by their nicknames. The Walking Tree (Dick Petrie), Bung Bung (Jack Barnett), Pisspot (Cyril Staple) and Ringer (Jim Gibson). The little gathering now under the verandah of the pub grew anxious as the time drew near. Not long now. The only question, when the double doors swung open, was who would break the ice and shamelessly stroll in first.

Opposite the pub was Flinders drapery and clothing store. Nearby, divided by a narrow alleyway stood Fred Gee Hong Yet's General Store. Fred now sat on a hard wooden stool with one knee tucked up against his cheek, foot on the seat, looking in total disgust at the rabble across the street.

Alec Younger sat near him. He was in the shade but still wore a flat, wide-brimmed felt hat. A long stem pipe sat squarely in his mouth. Puffs of smoke lay thick in the air. Grey, tailor-made trousers with respectable two-tone brown shoes completed his outfit. Alec was a frequent visitor to Wyndham. He was retired and used the state ships to travel between Darwin, Fremantle and places in between.

'Got money to drink!' old man Gee thought out loud. 'No pay me in shop. I catch him when he come back broke, hungry, looking for feed.'

His Chinese accent lay heavily on his chosen words. He could have been talking about all the blokes in the group. Most people would come good and pay up some time in the future. His real concern was his children, all young adults now and getting itchy feet. Which of them would stay and help in the business? He had three sons, Ernie, David and Morris. Two daughters, Edwina and Glenda. Already one of his daughters was attracting a lot of attention from a handsome young Italian meatworker.

At last the doors of the Wyndham Hotel were opened from within by the manager. In no time at all the footpath was deserted. Scrawny dogs stood gazing in through the open doors with tails wagging. No command from their masters. Two old black hounds picked the coolest spot. They flopped down and with bared teeth started to gouge the colony of ticks out from between their paws. It was going to be a long wait for the boss, and a longer one still for the next meal. Flies would be their only enemy unless Fred Gee Hong Yet's massive white bull terrier swaggered across the dusty street and decided on a little midday recreation.

Inside, the pub was quiet. Some serious drinking was under-way. You drank with your mate but this was no time for shouting. You drank within your means and at your leisure. Dave Rust could already feel his body responding. 'Up the British.' He threw one in for the old country. 'A man's got a right!' The bar was now insecure. 'Better grab a stool, bloody riding boots!' he cursed, stumbling. Anything to conceal his true state of inebriation.

Alan Donovan plodded up the front bar steps and paused. Tipping back his grey felt Akubra, he scratched his sweating forehead and looked around. 'Bloody hell, Dave! I didn't know you delivered your mob today!'

He was lying. Nothing got past Alan Donovan. He was the District Superintendent for the Public Works Department. His office and service buildings stood between the old school house and the police station. He saw the drovers pass through the town after making their delivery. He also noticed the head boy leading a riderless horse. He knew Dave Rust would be at the pub as soon as the sun threw a shadow on the yard arm.

'Strike me pink!' Alan grinned, the weedy, hand-rolled cigarette shuddering in his blackened teeth. 'You're pissed already, you bastard. I wanted to have a decent conversation with you, but I might have to wait till next year now!'

'Bullshit!' Two gnarled old hands met and locked in friendship. 'Grab a pew.' Dave was delighted. He looked around behind the bar. 'Where's the Silver Fox? You having the usual, Dizzy?'

Only friends called Alan that. They were two men, comparing notes, discussing the politics of the day, each genuinely interested in the economy and development in the vast Kimberley.

'Wally tells me it's a big kill this year. Better not say too much about the Karunjie bullocks, the grapevine's a bit savage.'

'Yes, yes,' Alan Donavan was quick with his gem. 'It's finally going to happen, all this talk about agricultural development on the Ord River. Pretty big stuff, I'm told it will be in two stages. First construction, a diversion dam on Bandicoot Bar. You know, the big watering hole below the night camp at Carlton Ridge bore. Not too far from where the Cockatoo Sands start.'

Dave listened hard. This was news indeed. Some years away for sure, but you could always tell when old Dizzy wasn't pulling your leg.

'Got the word,' Dizzy kept going. 'Have to send old Cyprian Birch and a couple of offsiders up to a place called Monsmon, just above the big dam site. Right now, no one can drive in from this end, too many bloody mountains. Durack's Folly's only good enough for donkeys and the likes of you, having the New York Jump-up experience. They have to go all the way to Argyle Station, turn west and follow a horse track over the hills into the valley. Gene French tells me you can't drive there, but old Cyp, despite his wooden leg, can drive anywhere. Need to have them stay for the full wet season, maybe more, so as to gauge the flow of the Ord flood. They'll be OK, a few rums and some good Argyle beef. No worries.' He was excited with the information he had in confidence. 'Going to be a bloody big dam, a lot of water. Then again, these young engineers reckon they know every bloody thing. Take away their theodolites and they'd run around like a blue-arsed fly.'

Dave took another sip. The publican took the cue and wiped the bar space dry while the small glass went almost to a horizontal position. At that moment, a din erupted; gurgling, yelping, howling and vicious snarling cracked the peace within. Immediately three blokes bolted to the door, cursing. Prime time interruption.

'Bloody dogs,' the publican broke his peace. 'The Roads Board should bring in some new laws. You'd think this was a black's camp. I don't know why we appointed Doak Matthews as the secretary. Never see him in the office. Always running around. Might be jealous of his pretty wife or showing off his new little Bedford utility.' A new rumour in the making, perhaps. He knew he had said too much, but he had chosen his words and listeners carefully.

'Yes, yes, yes,' Dizzy went on, unheeded. 'Might even be a big town out there somewhere near Ivanhoe. Trouble is, when they start something like that, especially a town, it gets filled with bloody wogs. Look at the meatworks, for example. Bloody United Nations every mealtime. Can't wait to get my own house away from there.'

This was Dizzy's usual tirade against the presence of those later to be known as 'New Australians'. By now Dave Rust was only up to an occasional 'Yeah' or 'Too right' or 'Bloody oath.'

'Don't look now,' Alan Donovan's eyes lit up. 'His Eminence is stretching his limits and visiting his flock in the front bar. He must be blind, magnifying specs and all. Only bloody billygoats here.'

Dave managed to turn on his stool. True enough, Bishop John Frewer was slowly moving from the lounge section towards them. 'Who knows,' he thought, 'what disappointment he goes through to try and bring a little divine comfort to the wicked of the earth. Bloody good bloke. Bloody fool!'

The Bishop, a genuine man of the cloth presented himself in his tropical regalia of pith hat, immaculate white shirt with tiny gold crosses on the lapels, cream short trousers with two sets of buckles at the high waistline and matching long socks. He steeled himself, took his last breath of purified air and approached the two Kimberley stalwarts.

'Good afternoon to you both,' he gracefully greeted them. 'I see you have already partaken of the cup on this wonderful day of our Lord.'

His smile broadened as he established his presence among the self-admitted sinners. Quietness came over the bar room. Then almost everyone started calling out or deliberately flashing a respectable nod. The gesture was made in hope that it would act as a barrier to prevent further conversation. But John Frewer knew his constituency well and was the proverbial expert at delivering a touch of heavenly disguised blessing. Take it or leave it.

It was Frewer's privilege to conduct ceremonies for the few faithful and the many who, for their own reasons, chose to live only in the false shadow of the cross. For him, the vision that motivated his inner self was clear; his difficulty was the translation of it for his sightless congregation in this wretched land. 'If I only had a building, a church and a bell to call this rabble together,' he thought as he gazed into the eyes of the untouchables, many a country mile from the golden gate. 'The House of the Lord God may even reign in Wyndham. In a little while at least, perhaps.'

The time dragged for those in the bar, all afraid to speak in case blasphemous interruptions fell out. 'Oh yes,' the Bishop spoke on his departure. 'There will be a service at the Mission House at six o'clock. See you all there! Yes? Yes? Yes?'

He delivered his last parting shot at Alan Donovan. But John

Frewer had many friends, nonetheless. His gentle conversation and presence provided a guarantee for all the gentry within the township of Wyndham. Apart from the Catholics, that is. If you were seen in his company, there was still spiritual hope. Everything that was genuinely of British breeding was associated with the Anglican Church. Church services, whether they were held at the Picture Gardens, the Mission House or on someone's backyard lawn, were a symbolic means for the European race to display its understanding of God and his kingdom.

The rituals of the service over, everyone was expected to pay their dues. Some were cursing their luck for not having smaller change when the Bishop came forth with his velvet clothed receptacle for the collection of offerings towards God's work in the district. Still, it was a small sacrifice to be accepted as the flock!

The Race Meeting

On the Saturday morning of the races Les Arthur positioned himself early. The pavilion was simple: four upright gum tree saplings with a heavy covering of tea-tree leaves for a roof. To strengthen the structure more saplings were wired with the usual Cobb & Co twitch halfway up on three sides. On the open front side, a small steel framed table with a pine board was topped with a hessian covering.

Les was seated in the small enclosure, which served as a ticketing box for the Wyndham race meeting. 'Hope the old girl doesn't spot the table when she comes later. Things will be right as long as the dog back home doesn't flatten the pot plants I took off it.' He reminded himself to replace it early in the morning. 'Bloody glass eye!' he cursed irritably as he delicately dabbed at the tears that seeped from under his dark craggy brow.

The mid-morning sun faced him now, but he had prepared for the afternoon's onslaught by placing more hessian bagging behind his construction. The only luxury was a conveniently placed thermos flask of hot tea. There was a great temptation to indulge in the amber fluid but he had to satisfy the missus with her constant nagging about booze and its effect, at least on the first day.

Already across the marsh at the Three Mile, the mirages were dancing. Aboriginal people walking the short distance from Gundagai looked grotesque, as their bodies appeared not to touch the ground and occasionally disappeared. There were trucks of all descriptions parked outside the crude fencing. Hundreds of people, mostly Aboriginal, completely covered these station vehicles. Everyone talked and laughed at once, all in anticipation of what would happen during that day and night. Dogs tied up under vehicles became disorientated and afraid, yelping and tipping over their given water supply. 'Die of thirst, you mangy, tick covered bastard, see if I care!' was the usual response.

Jim Boneham, or Tex as everyone called him, had his horse tied up out of the sun in the corner of the large bough shade stable. Horses now occupied most stalls with their handlers fussing over them. The whole course was built on the salt marsh. Every construction made of paperbark tree boughs looked the same, only the sizes differed according to their function. A canvas enclosure was placed all around the jockeys' pavilion to ensure privacy when changing and reduce the possibility of detection when debating how the race should be run, lost or won.

As the colonial gentry arrived in small groups, it was easy to detect the class distinction by their attire, paraded for all to see. Most women were adorned in pastel or white flowing dresses with stylish white embroidered floppy hats, white gloves, socks and shoes. Ladies from a more wealthy background were

143

bedecked in gold and long pearl necklaces. For those fortunate enough to have one, an umbrella added a touch of class. Men from the town's working class wore shorts with floral shirts, any old hat and sometimes a handkerchief knotted at every corner served just as well. Panama hats told you instantly the difference between townspeople and stock worker. If you wanted confirmation you would take a quick glance at who possessed bowed legs and R.M. Williams boots.

The Aboriginals provided a real splash of colour. Almost everyone had new clothing, hats and boots for the occasion. The women were decked out with large, multi-coloured large handkerchiefs over their heads, the whiteness of their teeth emphasised by their shining black faces. Little snotty nosed kids skidded around everywhere, some pretending to ride and fall off imaginary horses. No one told them to get out of the dust; the earth was of them and visa versa.

It was one time of the year when Aboriginal people mingled on the course, even though it was easy to spot that they sat apart from the rest. Those from stations sat on the ground, a good distance behind the stables outside the poorly fenced perimeter. If a horse lost control and bolted towards the line of people, an immediate shriek would erupt from women and children. They had nowhere to go, and could only huddle together and hope they would not be trampled.

The Aboriginal men on the other hand would not be so troubled. This was their trade, as it were. They would scramble to their feet and laughingly raise their hands and hats and call out 'Whoa! Whoa! Pull up!' while trying to grasp the flying, dragging reins. 'He right! He right! What you mob singin' out about. He knows us, this horse, he belong to old man our boss,' they would exclaim with added enjoyment. 'Look! Missus coming now. Might be horse been chuck him, old man! Poor bugger!'

After much cackling, everyone would settle down on the ground ready for the next turn of events. By two o'clock in the afternoon, the course would be alive with activity. The bookies would have had at least three races under their belts. Sam Thomas from Halls Creek would be perched on his half drum and calling odds on the next race. 'Only station hacks, grass fed hacks,' he conned away light heartedly. 'I'll take four to one!'

A large crowd of punters moved slowly around the group of bookies. Joe Mosey had another set of odds going and appeared to be attracting punters, but only the ones with deep pockets and short arms. The fervour increased as the jockeys, having completed the customary procedure in the mounting enclosure, now paraded their mounts directly in front of the spectator section, turning, then stiffly cantering down past the winning post.

Tex was having his usual problems with frightened, unsettled horses and was now leading one all the way around the course on the marsh. There was no conversation between riders as they gingerly rode out. Prancing horses sapped the strength of the small men mounted on their backs but they were mostly hard working individuals who possessed the stamina it required. For all of them, it was a bonus to ride.

'Might even crack a sheila at the ball at the Six Mile later. Better pull my guts in,' they would mutter to themselves, in anticipation that some thin-waisted flapper might have placed a bet on his mount and, should it win, she may want to reward him in private. They tried hard to not think about the race, but it was difficult. There was no barrier draw. 'Watch that bloody Joe Moore, look where he's got his nag, trying to get the jump on us, the cheeky bugger!'

'Come on, you buggers, line them up, haven't got all day.' Jack Martin, the starter took a swig of his bottle then tried to look serious as they came forward. Now in a much tighter grouping, ready for the open start at the drop of a flag, even the swearing had stopped. 'Here we go. Bugger!'

Famous last words. Back at the race grounds enclosure, the Wyndham crowd was hushed, all eyes west towards the mirage and blazing sunlight, now a moving splurge of a brown mass, topped with a mingling of many colours. Dust in the distance.

'They're off!' It came from a hundred different voices. Men ran from the bough shade bar with froth flying from bottled beer still clutched in their hands. 'Get out of my bloody way! Got money on this.' Their excuse to command a piece of the gum tree sapling railing. Ladies pranced up and down, slapping their gloved hands and screaming with delight at nothing in particular as they thought they recognised the sure thing some local expert had whispered, his pursed lips off the vertical flat of their palm. Anything to enhance their ten-shilling wager.

Like a huge Chinese festival dragon, the crowd along the rails gyrated amid cheers and screeches. The horses now appeared in full view on the two-furlong turn. As they galloped around, jostling for positions in the straight, the whips came out in earnest. From there, the crowd would bring them home as the dull drumming of the horses' hooves increased.

Within a hundred yards of the winning post, the inevitable was realised. There were screams of delight, quieter shameful mutterings of disgust, and unmentionable loud Australian adjectives from the most uncouth among the mob, all mingling on the salt marsh at Wyndham that afternoon as the dust blew in with the passing of the horses.

For Wyndham's urchins of the street—and now the race-course—there was no interest for horses or the people carrying out their annual ritual. But there were other opportunities. Loose mouths, loose hands and loose pockets. The kids strolled around with long sticks in their hands, flicking bottle tops, paper or anything that was lying around. They would be looking for lost coins and paper money. Down wind from the bookies was a good spot, just before the race when the old pound note was really on the move.

Two-up

Norm Dixon's spinning ginny roulette game attracted as many people as could squeeze in sideways at the table. In the afternoon the two-up game started and for some, the races were second place. Here was the real money. There was a big circle of men from all walks of life, all pursuing the one ambition: to be filthy rich and get out of this hole of a town. Dreams were won but mostly lost.

'Cover your bets now!' the caller piped up in a shrill voice. 'Lay them down on the ground, watch the wind!' He casually looked around. 'Don't be bashful, you blokes over there, dig deep and have a go. Some old horseshoes there to weigh your money down, the afternoon sea breeze is here.'

Old man Jim Neighbour nervously rubbed the white bristles on his unshaven face, his large red handkerchief hung conveniently over his shoulder. He was perspiring, masses of salty liquid running down the inside of his white pin-striped shirt. The caller looked in his direction. 'Come in spinner!'

Two new pennies lay on the sliver of pine in his large calloused hand. A steady glance at his hold, then he arched his body and, with a parting inward grunt, hurled the perfectly spinning coins into the air. 'Another set of heads,' he thought, 'and I'm sitting pretty.'

Casually the caller strolled to the middle of the large circle and looked down at the pennies. 'King bloody George and his twin!'

he confirmed. 'All right, you fellas on the side, clear your bets and set them up again.'

Quietly the Kimberley entourage responded. 'Shift your bloody dog, mate!' The caller looked after his clients. 'Only got a fiver in his hand,' he muttered in disgust. 'Don't go away, Jim. You're on mate.'

'Look that way!' an old bow-legged Aboriginal stockman exclaimed. 'Two fella ringer having a knuckle-up. By the livin'! Proper good fair go this one!'

People ran from everywhere to view the stoush under way. No one offered encouragement or called out. An unwritten rule. You may start something you can't finish.

Two well-proportioned stockman, bare-chested, stood toe to toe, landing blow after blow on each other. They fought behind the racecourse bar area, now completely surrounded by a mass of men. Some of these were nodding and acknowledging silent bets.

'These two are better than the last race. Any takers?' A gaunt looking lumper could not contain his excitement. 'Ten quid on the banger with the arse out of his trousers. Bit of a goer for me.'

A giant of a man standing behind spoke first. His voice came with an earthy but menacing intent. 'You're on!'

This was a cue for a number of invisible transactions from among the excited, intoxicated onlookers to reveal their preference by signalling their own bets. Water from the ice drums had leaked out on the salt marsh and created a wet area. Both men had slipped into this once or twice and were now splattered with mud, dust and blood. It was starting to get dirty. Up until now, several women who had a vantage point were enjoying the occasional glance of raw flesh and the sheer exhilaration of bloody combat. The brilliant late afternoon sun exposed the true colour of blood as it splattered under force and mingled with sweat and covered the heaving muscular chests of the young men. No backing down. 'Shit.'

Two women in particular had raised the fly veils from their perky little white hats, fanned themselves with gloves, emitted mewings and sweet little nothings and unashamedly commented to each other about the spasms that were taking place momentarily within their heavily breathing bodies. 'Look out!' someone called. 'Bloody coppers!'

The two men stopped instantly but continued to glare at each other. 'Another bloody minute and . . .'

'Yeah? Says who and with which bloody army?' the other bloke retaliated.

'Break it up!'

The sergeant finally shouldered his way through the crowd. He didn't have to say it but it was for the onlookers really. 'Bloody Wyndham Turf Club will kick the shit out of me,' he retorted. 'Got me timing wrong here, and missed a beauty too? Come on fellas!' He stretched to his full height of six foot, four inches and noticed the effect it had. 'Get your shirts on and try to behave. I catch you two piss farts at this stunt once more, just showin' off the pair of you, and I'll have both in the bloody slammer for the whole week.'

He waited for it to sink in. 'They're pissed,' he thought. 'But if I started with these two in the first day of the races, I won't have any room by Monday. Anyway, who's going to feed them? I want to watch the races myself!'

'Get out of my sight, get to your camps and don't show your ugly snouts until tomorrow.' The victory was his. 'Show's over!'

He needed a drink just like everyone else.

'Bugger!' The exclamation resounded throughout.

Mid-afternoon, the sea breeze was already blowing stronger and becoming uncomfortable at that. Swirling dust reminded everyone that Wyndham was on the salt marsh. Flies stung when they bit, every scratch burned with salt. Salty liquid in the corners of every eye. Little children were fast asleep, lying half on, half off ground sheets in the shade. Even some old grannies had called it a day. The kids would poke fun at them as they spotted some snoring, mouths open, exposing false teeth, completely overwhelmed by tiredness. Grandfathers had already taken the opportunity and sneaked off to the rowdy bar and two-up den.

Another dogfight shifted the screaming kids and the chairs. A station owner sunk his riding boot into the ribs of the biggest dog. End of story.

A mother was getting worried. She had noticed her fourteen-year-old daughter and a new-found girlfriend making eyes at two young men of a similar age from the station. Both were over-dressed in their gear. Shirts were too large and sleeves rolled all the way up to the collarbone. The hats were new but did not fit and caused the ears to bulge out like apes'. Young fellas had been talking about this occasion all year. A jackeroo had laughingly told them, 'You larrikins are all hats, boots and bloody balls. If you snagged one of those town sheilas, you wouldn't know what to do with them.'

They laughed, knowing it was mostly true but hoping someone would tell them more. The sun would go down soon, and the race meeting was really a time and a place to talk, to learn, to gain and who knows, perhaps a new opportunity or desire would be achieved. If not, there was always next year. 'Shit!'

Big Corroboree

Just before sundown, despite the races still being in progress, a different issue altogether was developing among the Aboriginal people. The word had already been passed around. 'Big corroboree, not far from that Territory mob camp. Lot of Territory blackfellas been come. Got a new dance. Some proper Lawmen there too. Young fella and young girl can't get too cheeky tonight. Them old women, going to dance proper way too, look out! Might be we see some young women with shining, standing up tit like boab nut. Them young men who dancing gonna proper show off tonight with their hair belt and tight cock rag. The dust is going to fly tonight.'

This was to be no coincidental gathering. When young men go to great extremes to flick dust with the flying movement of toes and feet it automatically sends out signals of another kind. It simply means: ' See my capability, I have control of the earth. The earth is my mother, my being. I present it to you. See my body. Watch, gloat and receive. With caution, a risk, you and I could perhaps share something later!'

No shade, open space. The dancers would be ready behind an enclosure made of boughs covered with a pall of hazy smoke and dust. Nothing unusual. Late afternoon sun glared across the mudflats, taking its toll on the dancers, already daubed in beautiful red and white ochres. Sweat causing minute streaks through the paint, the men stood motionless, waiting for their moment, blood already pounding in the bulging veins of their exposed bodies. There was a good-sized pile of wood between the designated dance area and the assembled group of dignified singers. When darkness eventually came, it would be lit.

The men and women drank steadily from battered old billycans of water. It was their responsibility to sing the inspirational songs, accompanied with the didgeridoo and tap sticks. Dancers, men and women with young children joined in on various occasions, with energetic movement and body control that entertained the crowd.

Boisterous challenges would come from the spectators to perform an impossible step or twist. Most times, someone would

151

take it up. It was always easy to pick these young men. Lithe, slow, prancing, cheeky and challenging, eyes not always in the direction they should be. The women were equally provocative. Their eyes were always lowered yet their body and foot movements were presented vigorously to new admirers that they may have come into contact with just that day.

This was a supreme display. Better than the wet weather walkabout, it was an opportunity to view the prospects of the field beyond your intended. Young men gaped and swallowed hard. But this was no sordid, lurid, flesh-revealing displaying of paganistic rituals. As each song was sung and every participant presented their utmost, it was almost a personal song, personal dance, presented to the mesmerising spirits that controlled Indigenous destiny. A time of spiritual love. A time of personal love. A time of being there. A time of understanding. A time of knowing. A time of tranquillity. A time when Aboriginal people could cry and be thankful.

Grey haired old grannies sat in a tight group close to the old men. Tears crept from their pursed eyes as they commenced their performance with harmonious precision. Smoke and the salt marsh dust caused only a slight quaver in the divine concert to the ancient spirits. From coarse old lips came the last, long, lingering sounds.

They all paused. Aged, gnarled fingers grasped the tap sticks and then began the sharp, clear rhythm. Simultaneously the women with cupped hands beat the deep muffled sound on their inner thighs. It was the 1950s—but it could have been five centuries earlier.

A voice called out from within the jumbled orchestra sitting together for warmth on the ground. 'Fetch him up water, quick fella! This didgeridoo still too dry.'

Some of the audience laughed at this interruption as the

women began again as one. The opening note was high-pitched, startling, and caused the crowd to hush. A new sequence of song, a pause in between each presentation of ghost-like dancers, then, on a silent command, the women quickly turned their bodies and moved behind the leafy enclosure.

A brief interlude to wet the throat and suck in breaths of the cool evening air. Old aching bones would need to be stretched. Sufficient time to shift the soggy ball of tobacco from one side of the mouth to the other. A quick wet gurgling spit to clear the residue of accumulated saliva and the dark nicotine juices. Some poor child would always be in the way. The grandmother would scold the child for being on her lap. No response at all, this was security at its best. A long night ahead.

As the mass of dark bodies moved and mingled, impatient for the next dance, someone in the crowd deliberately, loudly, broke wind. Instant laugher and hilarious exclamations in several different languages, everyone jokingly blaming each other. A harsh reprimand from an old painted elder brought everyone back to reality; there were serious cultural matters to attend to. There was now only a dull red glow in the west. Darkness comes quickly in the tropics. Children playing in the dust were the only ones who had not noticed the temperature change. Fires were being stoked. Dogs had lost the urge to respond to foreign odours. The smell of food was wafting through the air and dust. Time for a feed and a change of singers and dancers.

New mob! Look out now!

A group of Aboriginal men appeared out of nowhere. Already symbolically marked in vivid white ochre and a burnt red like the very rocks of the Kimberley, they moved slowly among the rest. Wide-eyed children quickly made space and turned to their mothers for security. The messengers carried huge bundles of ochre-coloured bamboo. This ritual was called Wunan. It was a traditional distribution of wealth, a bartering. A means of caring and sharing. Aboriginal currency.

In earlier days, in the traditional way, it would take several years for the final distribution of wealth to all of those eligible. But travel to the race meetings, all the way across the country, assisted by modern transport systems, allowed this ancient ritual to occur more often. Years earlier, missionaries of various Christian faiths, wishing to eradicate so-called heathenism and Indigenous ignorance, had recognised the symbolism of the Wunan system, and exerted great effort in destroying spears, boomerangs and any other articles traded from far reaching locations. Once the cultural connection was severed the rest would be easy. Total dependence on the mission and a spoon-fed culture would rapidly condemn the Indigenous way to oblivion.

'Don't walk around!' a middle-aged Aboriginal man warned his two sons and their mate. 'They been say 'Goodatji Goodatji' here too. Look out for Feather Foot!'

The concerned look that accompanied his warning was sufficient. It was immediately heeded.

The moon was approaching its first quarter, not enough light to discern shadows and movement. You couldn't be too careful. A group of young women standing away off in the open ground left only thin fleeting shadows. They laughed loudly and suggestively, signalling their whereabouts. If only the right person in the right group would respond. On the first day of the races at the Three Mile, these lithe young women would have put on socks and sandals and multi-coloured beads, hairpins and bangles to attract their fancy. Too much was at stake to talk to these muscular, white toothed larrikins from all over the Kimberley in full view of the mob. Now at night it would be different; all were on equal ground. The concealed smile, the straight back, the uplifted breasts, swaying hips and the way they sat, signalled, 'Later, sun go down. Somewhere, might be!'

Some old granny would see the signs and next day analyse the results of the night's rendezvous. Who knows, it may even carry over until the next wet season. 'Might be big fight, might be somebody runaway, might be two fella fetch him up piccaninny.'

'Yella fella walkin' round tonight. Grab them silly bugger, can't look out proper way! Got no earhole!'

'Them yella fella make their own Dreaming! Cunning bastard!'

Aboriginal girls and women were so vulnerable. How sad! Again a granny's wise warning. Experience had taught the older women and made them cautious; they knew what to expect from this fast changing world. Many had silently endured a life of hidden shame, enticed by certain things, only to be caught between two ways of life on the stations.

On the Station

No one spoke a word of rebuke about the half-caste child born down the camp back on the station. The unfortunate child, born out of wedlock, the yellow bastard was sometimes the result of a planned union between a giggling, inquisitive, beautiful young Aboriginal woman and a handsome strong jackaroo, up from the big smoke. His first job, and most likely his first woman. Both innocents in the big picture, both only responding to their desires.

The kitchen was a trap for those who had washing up duties after supper in the big house. Depending on the attitudes and intentions of the boss, sometimes he struck up a quick friendship with a middle-aged Aboriginal stockman. They would pair off when mustering with the mob; the boss would offer him some rollings from his tin of Log Cabin tobacco. Might have even given him an old whip. This was a sign of distinction among Aboriginal stockmen, the ultimate symbol of acceptance. Too late, the

Aboriginal man would realise his dilemma. It was a big decision to make, whether to acknowledge and capitalise on this new privilege, or stay in his former tribal position. When he finally noticed the widening gap between him and his much younger wife who worked within the big house complex, it was too late. The boss would not have to say a word, or do anything. Such things were well known on the station but never discussed. Black velvet.

Old men who had status in the Aboriginal community were often whisked away and placed in humiliating roles on the stations. All day, they would be without contact from everyone else, forced to care for goats, the station garden and various wood heaps, enticed away by a little extra stick of tobacco or a second-hand pair of boots, a belt. Sometimes it was only a smile and an arm around the shoulder.

The Aboriginal people believed in body contact as a show of affection. They took kind gestures for granted in those early days, not understanding the new society's way at all. 'Two fella, missus and boss, proper good poor buggers!'

Most Aboriginal people would stay on stations throughout this era. It was true! Right across the Kimberley were genuine individuals who had come through the school of hard knocks. They earned their rightful place in a growing industry in what was a rotten, harsh environment for people with a Caucasian ancestry. Most young white men who were adventurous went out and flaunted with death. You either burnt yourself out, got yourself killed or turned out to be a spit and polish horse tailer, a cook who could cook and fight as well. Or you married the boss' daughter because you could ride, handle stock and could also fight, and you were ambitious, earned your keep and could back yourself up in any situation to boot.

'Missus, no more catch him up, boss!' Aboriginal women would remark.

This meant a number of things. The boss, usually a stockman who had worked his way through the sodden dust and cow-dung splattered ranks, had quickly sought a bride to establish himself as a man of renown and responsibilities. The new missus was often still young and, coming from a completely different or vague background, would have extreme difficulty fitting in and understanding her husband's role. He would be embarrassed, totally unsympathetic and overwhelm her with responsibilities. She would be left in charge of the station home and be responsible for the natives, who knew little of the big house protocol and had to be coaxed and cajoled into performing standard tasks. Everyone learnt from each other. Way to go! There were also many women, equally as adventurous as their male counterparts who had the skills and enthusiasm to embark on a lifestyle still in its early stages and yet to be given a name.

'Who that new missus?' old Aboriginal women would ask.

Someone already up to date with the latest news would answer. 'He not missus! Might be, by and by!' There'd be laughter. 'Look out! He proper ki-eye (a flirt) bugger that one, too young, that ngaringa (young Aboriginal woman).' (The Gidja language was understood along all East Kimberley stock routes.)

'Don't like that,' someone might say. 'The new governess, lookin' after kid for two fella boss.'

These young white women, as history would show, were the answers to everyone's prayers, from the boss, right through to the station's Aboriginal community. Without a doubt. These young flowers of Australia came as budding governesses, teachers, nurses, jillaroos, bookkeepers, students. They became lovers, wives, accountants, artists, landowners, bosses, shire presidents, midwives, mothers, grandmothers, authors, graves in the never never.

'I been talk to missus today, what you reckon? Flying doctor coming next week. Doctor going to talk to us!' The old Aboriginal lady spoke, not knowing if her discussion with a concerned boss' wife would have any results. She spoke again. 'Me no more liar! You fellas look out now! No more bullshit! Too many piccaninny sick, lice longa hair! Gutsache, old man got buggered-up leg and back from horse and bullock.'

No one responded. It was their misfortune not to have the vocabulary to supply their answers.

The old Aboriginal lady walked away towards her humpy and waiting family. Small fires glowed everywhere. Smoke hung in the hollows and mingled with dust kicked up by children as they playfully spent their energy. From the outer west end side of the blacks' camp came the distant mournful song of old men. Old women knew the signs of lament, but in the camp, their responsibility was survival. They would satisfy their grief with a long drifting gaze through the jumbled, cramped campsite. 'Poor fella! My country!' Their satisfaction would come later. 'After bullock work finish, wet weather come up and everybody go bush.'

Then, secret women's business!

Booze Up

The western horizon was a dull red. The quarter moon, now low in the evening sky, shed a dim ghostly light. Dust hung over the numerous camps, the glow of many fires clearly silhouetting hectic movement. The town had not yet gone to sleep. Everyone had another venue in mind.

The noise level at the Six Mile Pub was gradually building. Stock people of all descriptions packed the hotel, the majority taking all the standing room at the bar side. Most had had a skinful at the races and had merely come here for seconds and what the bush picnic had to offer. Tobacco smoke hung the same thickness all the way from floor to the ceiling, a camouflage for the many groups of grizzled old campaigners with battered hats and scarred faces. One could hardly call these characters gentlemen. Many had not washed other than their hands and faces since making damper early that morning. The first two bottles of rum or whisky had gone down post-haste, their tongues had been sour and their mouths stank. They were resigned to the fact that no town sheila was going to fall over in front of them with silks at half-mast and legs askew. 'Anyway, be back at the station next week. My piece of black velvet will always be there!'

Craps Mallon and Roger Percival sat apart by themselves, the empty bottle before them. Both good mates, same habits, unmarried in the European sense, without eye contact, both defying each other to fork out for the next charge. 'The old shit!' Craps thought, 'He knows I bought the last shout last year! Just because he's the boss. I'll check on his movement in the station kitchen in the future. Old bastard!'

A muster of stockmen and young managers occupied the middle section of the bar. The usual conversation. When the races were happening the pub was the only opportunity for horse owners, jockeys and influential people to meet.

These people of the Kimberley held a limited conversation. Stations that paid a good quid, horses that could buck like Curio, sheilas, black, white or brindle, that had the smell and the look, managers and stockmen that could fight, big mobs of bullocks and droving trips. Now and then someone would brag about a droving trip to railheads in sunny Queensland. It would not last long as Top Enders were patriotic and would notoriously defend their patch. If, however, a Queenslander was in the company, and it was often, a typical blue developed, out of sheer competition, nothing else.

There was little love lost between men from different states. If the difference was obvious, then everyone bought drinks and went outside to settle the dispute in the Australian manner. If the accusing parties were mates, then the question would be settled in a test of strength. Either arm wrestling or scratch pulling, both might prove you weren't as strong as your opponent but still left you a man, a worthy competitor.

'Heard a bloke say that a young yella fella flogged the shit out of you at the Linnekar races, a while back! That true?' a tall, thin horse tailer with a broken nose said to a young and handsome Harold McNamara.

Harold, in response, shifted his hat forward and lower over his face, his dark eyebrows revealing uncertainty. Put on the spot, he was obliged to clear the air as every new and battered Akubra slowly turned in his direction. He stood his full height, made sure he presented his biceps to their full potential and spoke. 'You want to hear the full story or do you want to hear the bullshit the cook spat out after a drop of white lady (tea and methylated spirits).'

Under pressure, the ringer looked around. 'You know me, mate. Only asking. Spill your guts.'

'Well, anyway,' Harold resumed, 'this young half-caste, Tim Kelly was his name, walked up to the bar at the Linnekar and asked for a beer. No blackfellas, as you all know, were being served there. White man's country only. You had to be quarter-caste and from the Northern Territory to score a sniff.

'Anyway, this bloke came from the south of Western Australia, a decent shit kicker, meant no harm and only had a thirst. Poor bastard! The grog suppliers asked him to leave, somebody called him a bloody boong, and it was on. I was having a drink under the enclosure at the other end and watched him walk away. He didn't go too far, turned around, called us all the white shits

160

under the Southern Cross and challenged anybody to have a go at the black Aussie.'

McNamara let that sink in then went on. 'I ran me blinkers over him and noticed he was short, an axe handle across the shoulders. Powerful arms of a yard builder. 'Shit!' I thought. 'What's gonna happen here?'

'Would you believe nobody moved? Some of you fellas may have been there. Anyway, that's on your gutless shoulders.' Harold had their full attention now. 'I looked around and thought, a whole bough shade full of them and not a real white man in sight. A bunch of bloody geldings, that's for sure!'

Everyone was listening so Harold, now with pride, glided into the nasty bits of yet another Kimberley legend.

"Over here!' I called out to him. 'Don't know your gripe, but I'm a white man! Up your bloody arse!'

Tim Kelly knew that when he offered the challenge to the bar, he was angry, but then in the silence, with all eyes upon him, he was prepared to accept the worst. 'I'll be happy if I flatten one or two, then get away! Quick smart! There's no bullshit here. It's fair dinkum stuff now,' he thought. When he heard the voice of the big-boned muscular Kimberley stockman as he stepped out of the mass of hats, boots, belts and gabardine gear, he was relieved. 'If I lose,' he thought, 'It's my fault! I'll go down in style! The odds are even!'

Tim Kelly looked at Harold MacNamara, a Kimberley white man, a six-footer, all bone and muscle. 'Give it a go,' he thought. 'One man at least, make me feel a little better.'

'Tell you what,' Harold McNamara wound up the story with a toss of his black Akubra. 'I said to him, 'My jeep's parked over there. Not going to give these gutless mongrels the benefit of the doubt. You and I discuss this man's business somewhere else, out in the flat where the bulls feed and the best man drives back here again. Okay? ' 'Fair enough!' Tim agreed.

'Twenty minutes later, Tim Kelly drove the Lissadell Station jeep into the Linnekar racecourse. I was in the passenger seat, slightly concussed, a bit chewed up where it matters most, but obviously the biggest white man in the district.'

It was about that time of the night. Norman Bridge had reached his peak. He was doing a little foot tapping and dancing around. The mouth organ was out and chirping away at some melodious ditty that most people knew and were joyfully slaughtering. Happy, happy, happy! It was a shame there was no one to play the bloody spoons.

A big ringer had stumbled outside into the night air. His calculations were simple. 'I've had enough, grab one for the road and call it a day. Me swag's in a good spot. There's a bit of skirt, old Mick's daughter, a bit of coloured truffle, she won't be chasin' no blackfella tonight! She knows me, she might be waiting!'

Outside, yet another saga was developing. The bonnet was up on the old grey Austin truck from Texas Downs Station. Somebody up shit creek! To keep the petrol clean was a hard task in the Kimberley's dusty environment. 'I've cleared out the carbie,' the fat old driver commented. 'Got to get going before the bloody coppers come. Bloody Wilhelm, copper bastard!' He turned to the big ringer just moving out through the doorway. 'Can you give us a crank, mate? I need to have a boot on the revs. Jimmy Klein will sack me if he knows what I'm up to with his truck.'

'Blood' oath, mate!' the ringer replied.

He put the full bottle of Beenleigh on the channel iron bullbar, locked the crank handle on the dog, turned the motor until he had full compression, then took the first full swing. The bottle containing the rest of the night's entertainment toppled over and shattered on the stony driveway. Almost instantly, the ringer bellowed and cursed with disgust, withdrew the crank handle and threw it into the dark.

The old man behind the wheel muttered, 'Shit!' He was instantly committed to sharing his grog; his hands groped hurriedly under the seat and found the peacemaker. 'She'll be right mate! Here, take mine,' he quickly stammered. Cursing his luck, he handed over the full bottle, still sealed. But at least now his parched features would remain intact a little longer. The original problem still not solved, he would most likely use up all of his wax matches looking for the lost crank handle in the castor oil bushes.

Back in the bar Jack Doby, cook of renown, but unfortunately an alcoholic of equal renown, staggered out into the night's cool air. He had called the publican's bluff for two hours now before being finally asked to leave. No matter that money talked all languages and crossed all barriers, he had his last wish granted and wrapped in brown paper. His horn-rimmed glasses intact and perched on his massive flowing crop of silver hair, Jack called it a night. His grey flannel, collarless shirt was blotched with wine-stained wet patches from below his large sagging jowl to his bulging belly. As he left the security of the bar, three locals immediately occupied his vacated space. Jack Doby stank something awful and nearby patrons nodded gratefully to the equally relieved licensee, Jack Woodland, behind the bar. If this were daytime, Doby would have been followed by a swarm of flies all focused on his arse end.

As he stiffly marched to the double outer doors of the pub, he realised that he had already pissed himself. No one had noticed. A re-enactment of race three was being carried out by Joe Moore. As everyone participated, acting out the events that brought the horse home, Jack had conveniently urinated in his oversized Bombay bloomers, then squelched towards the door in his stained, sockless sandshoes. Bloody hell!

The Bull Pen

Outside, Jack Doby had regrets. Where was he going to camp for the night? This was a new decade with new management. Previous partners in the Six Mile Pub, Arthur Bruton and Archie Martin, had succumbed to pressure from the Roads Board and the Police Department and had done away with the bull pen. Doby would have no alternative but to collapse outside, clutching his bottle of Invalid port and hoping the police would have compassion and deliver him back to his camp. This time he would wake before dawn, dry-mouthed and without his reviver!

The bull pen had been a house of convenience, a shelter that stood in front of the old pub between the two boab trees that are still there today. It was a typical old shed with a tin roof, dirt floor and vertical stripped bamboo slats. It contained about fifteen old steel cyclone bunks with coconut husk mattresses. Its purpose was the preservation of its clientele. The pound sterling was in short supply and pastoral companies only paid with valid cheques. The cheques were honoured by all business establishments. The publicans would not see their annual customers fleeced of their worldly resources and pastoral connections. Upon arrival in Wyndham, after the first drinks and exclamations of 'Allah be praised,' or 'Up yours' or 'God bless Ireland' or 'Forever England', the next discussion would be 'Watch me guineas, Arthur! There's a quid in it for you, mate.'

We saw it all, we lived there, under a bauhinia tree behind the pub.

Any old drunk whose source of ancestry was Great Britain or was accepted as such could sleep it out at the pen. They were all there. Heaps of them! Beds full. All drunk, sleeping off a binge that would continue as long as their cheques would last, sometimes for weeks on end. Shit and piss all over the place! Vomit, on the floor, on the beds, on the bodies of the pioneers of this country.

Laurie, my older brother would lead, and we would hide in the castor oil bushes behind the old building. We would peep inside and take in the scene.

In peak season, usually times of race meetings and cattle deliveries to the meatworks, the bull pen would be full. Drunks on every available surface. Covered with flies and mosquitoes, we thought sometimes they were dead. Some ringers would still be dressed in the clothes they turned up in days before, army great coats, boots and all. Some were half-clothed or had no clothes at all. It was a shock for us to see all those red faces, pure white skins and the grotesque, wrinkled genitalia hanging out for all to see, balls and all. It frightened us, this white man's world. If that was what the British Empire was like, we were totally confused. Home of drunks, home of people from England.

The mornings would always be peaceful. Arthur Bruton and Archie Martin would by now have finalised their calculations of the designated earnings. Dad and Mum would be cleaning the hotel. We kids would be casually patrolling the grounds in search of lost articles, with the intention of passing any discovery on to our parents. Money was no good to us, it had no value. Who would take pennies or silver coins from dark children? We had virtually no status in the community. Our parents were on the bottom of the proverbial ladder. It was true. It was as if us kids did not exist.

Stolen Piccaninny

Stolen Piccaninny

Song of the Ord

What have they done to our river
Dear bringer of life on the land
Once so majestic and awesome
Now choked, congested and shamed
Visions of a free, wild river
Roaring, brown in its quest
Still torments our memory
We saw it at its best

We do not know man's ambitions
To conquer and rape the land
To build what he knows is unnatural
And desecrate with his own hand
Nevertheless our river is existing
Fat and bloated in girth
We should be condemned and buried
For changing the Spirit's own earth

Again we see the river
Too shame to call it by name
An inkling of its former beauty
No more will it be the same
Do we not see the harm we bring
Blinded with fortune and fame
It's our river were dealing with
When it's gone, it's gone, the shame

We few who carry on Dreaming
See a beautiful Utopia in view
Of placid pools in seasons
Untouched by me and you
Our river, my river, I miss you
Place of knowledge and youth
Give us a meaningful respite
You are not yet beyond rebirth

Abduction

Many times Mum told us her sad story. She could never erase it from her mind. It had been such a traumatic experience.

To our best estimates the following events occurred somewhere around 1910 to 1912 when my mother was about six or seven years of age. She was with her mother, part of a large tribal group on their traditional home ground pastoral, a property in the Northern Territory. The bush camp was peaceful; there was no indication of the impending disaster.

Station managers knew there were so-called half-caste children, 'running' in the bush with the blacks. Usually they informed the local police, who then had the responsibility of 'rescuing' these children from a 'pagan' lifestyle, thereby giving them a chance at 'real life'. Mum and her people weren't to know that their tribe had been stalked by a police contingent from Turkey Creek (now Warmun) in Western Australia.

It was towards the end of the wet season. The majority of the Aboriginal people from the cattle station were still camped out in the bush a good distance from the homestead. Thoroughly enjoying the benefits of the bush and all it had to offer in regards to food, space and culture, they did not expect what would happen next.

At daybreak they came galloping in, mounted police and trackers, whitefellas and blackfellas, firing shots in the air. They could have been looking for individual miscreants such as cattle killers as well, for they came in with intent. My grandmother, Mary Boonay from the Mirriwoong/Marlngin people, made her escape quick and easy. She effortlessly scooped up Mum's younger brother Ben in one strong arm. With the other, she grabbed Mum's hand and headed up a deep narrow gully at a frantic pace. Some distance from the camp, she spotted a large old gum tree. Its trunk had been burnt as a result of lightning strikes and was hollowed; the base offered a hiding place. Granny Boonay needed to catch her breath and rest the children. With a warning to Mum and little Ben to stop crying and be quiet, they all squeezed in and waited.

Down at the camp the melee had ceased. But out in the bush, the search continued for those 'yella piccaninnies'. Some of our people had escaped, frightened, not knowing what to expect. Their very act of running away, however, implied guilt, albeit for unknown, uncommitted crimes. But most did not run; they were station blacks and were only on walkabout from the station work. Wet weather blackfellas!

Daylight came fast. The keen eyes of the black tracker picked up the giveaway signs. Granny Mary Boonay had every reason to run. She knew the police wanted her offspring. She had long known that one day they would be taken, but not today, not if she had the opportunity to prevent it. Her children had been given whitefella names, Polly and Ben. That missus from the station told her, 'Don't take those kids bush, Mary. Give them a chance. You know what will happen to them, especially that little girl. Leave them here. You can stop too, you been here at the station camp for a good while, you know what happening to all the blackfellas now. That policeman from Turkey Creek been talking to boss, and boss been tell him already.' She also tried to frighten her. 'You've got to look out for them Afghan camel drivers, they know everybody, they always looking for young girl, they bad buggers them lot. You know.'

The manager's wife did have real compassion for my grand-mother and her dilemma. She tried hard to convince her to give over to the inevitable. She made clothes for the kids, she even talked to them, poor little buggers. No one had predicted there was going to be this kind of trouble—'yellow bastards' springing up all over the place. I can imagine she made a promise to herself to diligently watch her husband, the manager, and secretly observe his body language and attitudes, especially when the blacks were working around the place. 'You really couldn't trust some of these young gins,' she must have thought to herself.

The missus probably hoped too that she herself didn't get sick, otherwise she would have to go south for treatment. It would be better to go on holidays together with her husband. She had left him alone on the station last wet. Already there could be the possibility of a little yellow bastard that looks like him hanging around the station and the blacks camp. What would the family in Queensland think if that happened?

The perspiration had dried on my granny's quivering body. She was still cold. She looked at her children, fearful of what would happen next. She was frightened of the whitefella and what he represented. Granny had already heard of stories of half-caste children taken, gone forever, and then family cry for a long time. Even so, she had no real inkling of the extreme repercussions of her children being stolen from her.

She did not hear the sound of the horses' hooves muffled in the sandy base of the gully. It was too late! The harsh voice of the tracker shocked her into reality. 'They there, boss! Them two fella piccaninnies, that gin there too. They been knock up early, can't get away from horse.'

Call it what you like. Superiority, conquering attitude, colonial system. My people suffered. My granny cried a thousand times from this moment. Heart wrenching hurt, beyond measure. Many believed then that Aboriginal people were not capable of love or human emotion. Aboriginal mothers only had instincts like animals; they were not gifted with the sensitivity of a Caucasian female towards her brood. It was even recorded thus in parliament.

'Grab that girl first,' the policeman directed. 'I think that other kid too small, still on the tit. Leave him with the lubra, catch him up by and by.'

Mary Boonay started wailing, knowing the inevitable, too scared to resist. 'Waah! Waah!' She was almost fainting. 'This white man no good,' she uttered in her own language.

The black tracker roughly grabbed the little girl, wrenched her fiercely from Mary Boonay.

'Gone. No touch. My child. Waah! Waah!'

Granny resorted to her native tongue, Mirriwoong/Marlngin

language, to console herself in her moment of grief. But there were no words adequate to describe the obscene situation. Her hurt was indescribable, her mind unable to contain this unthinkable inhumane act. Her body became numb and quivering, her eyes glazed. A spirited presence momentarily received her mortal body.

All this time, my Uncle Ben, then only a little child, was howling his head off, not knowing what was happening. It was he who snapped his mother into reality. Through tearful eyes, she saw her daughter Polly astride the saddle in front of the white policeman. She was being taken away. Down the eroded gully, out of sight. Away! Away!

Country Longway Behind

My mother cried. She could not understand what had happened. She was given food and something new and sweet to her taste. The policeman had said if she were good all the time, she would be given more of the good stuff wrapped in paper. First it was tomahawks, beads, flour, sugar and salt. Then tobacco and beef. Now it was boiled lollies, sweet but bitter.

The police contingent traveled to Mistake Creek, on to Spring Creek and then towards Turkey Creek Police Station in Western Australia. My mother sat on a pack mule for most of the journey, oblivious of the distance, unaware of the pain, the last stark image of her mother and brother imprinted in her mind. Nothing fitting together. Nothing making any sense. Misery was upon her. Her face streaked with tears each day, she rarely saw the sombre group at her rear, chained and walking behind the horse, ridden by one of the police boys. The other brought up the rear guard. Whilst on their patrol in the East Kimberley and Territory, the police had also gathered up Aboriginals suspected of crimes and they were now were being force-marched westwards. Some were relatives. My mother cried for them as well.

The chains wore heavily around their necks and they all strode in unison, so as to ease the continuous jolting and the mutilation of their flesh. Their arms cramped after holding the weight of neck braces. Mile after mile of an endless, bleeding journey. Flies, pain, thirst. Some showed signs of extreme stress but this was of no consequence to the constabulary. The prisoners would be marched until their bodies succumbed to these pressures. If one died, his body would be released from the neck braces and dumped where it fell, covered with stones. Soon crows, carrion, meat-ants and time would erase all record of life and the crime against humanity.

Somewhere in my mother's oblivion, they crossed a big river, the Ord, a thing of beauty in those days. 'That river go long way. Close up Wyndham, then saltwater. Might be we catch him up by and by,' the police boy told her that day.

Turkey Creek: a police station, a post office and a blackfellas' camp. That was all. Here my mother met Julia, a little girl, younger, but now wise to events. She was already taken away from her black mother, never to return, never to have a choice. These were Gidja people, with a culture and a language that was foreign to that of little Polly's now distant family. She continued to cry, her heart always on the verge of breaking.

After some days the camel dray came. Noisy, belching and ugly, the camels flopped down at the Afghan teamster's command. They were traveling light, returning from the Halls Creek goldfields. As usual, they would graze in the horse paddock at the police station, the camel bells, a monotonous, clanking tinny sound, annoying all night. The driver had learned, after his meal of salt beef, damper and bush figs that he had another yella kid to take to Wyndham. As well, the Aboriginal prisoners, nearly forty in number, would be chained to his dray and be made to walk behind, over the rocky rugged ranges all the way to Wyndham on the Cambridge Gulf. The policeman would ride in escort. They had caught some real bad buggers this time, he said.

After the court case in Wyndham, the driver would have a decent meal in the pub and a secluded grog-up with the local constabulary. It did not pay to display your weaknesses to the colonial gentry who could capitalise on anything. Every drover, miner or town layabout in town would have known of the arrival of the mounted policeman, his charges and the Afghan camel team. The copper had contacts all over the Kimberley; every station owner and manager was his ally. As representative of the monarchy, he could not afford to openly partake of alcohol as he might have wanted. The only safe place was the station and lock-up area, a sly drink with his policeman colleagues. If any locals or bushies spotted him and noted a special brand of alcohol or a choice brand of tobacco, then that information was carried for future bribes against any charges of common misdemeanours that might be committed. It was known that coppers' attitudes changed from time to time. Policemen were always hand-picked for the job and were backed up with one or two black trackers. But God help the unfortunate bastards who could not shape up. There are many unmarked graves, boot soles and heels, belt buckles, tobacco tins and empty .44 calibre cartridge shells in the dust between Wyndham and Halls Creek. Relics of many untold stories.

Ah Kim's

Now the copper, the trackers and the camel driver were ready to set off again. The journey to Wyndham resumed. It would be just as difficult as the previous stage for my mother. Boiled lollies again the only respite.

At last the camel dray and its entourage plodded up to Ah Kim's Store and vegetable gardens on Parry's Creek, about twenty-two miles from Wyndham. The policeman halted the miserable looking caravan in the shade. Affected now by the plight of the bush natives, the Afghan untied two large flat-sided billycans, filled them with cool creek water and offered the prisoners a long drink. Some were completely exhausted. With glazed eyes, others were singing softly to themselves in their native tongue, the lyrics haunting reminders of a land they might never see again.

'Come on, girl. This is where you get off,' the policeman said to my mother. He reached up to the dray for her hand. 'Leave that blanket there, the old Chinaman's got plenty.'

The little girl was compliant, and that was good. He was her only chance of survival. Besides, there was hardly a tear left in her shrunken, quivering body. Her eyes followed every movement around her.

'Here, get on the horse. The sand in the creek's too bloody hot.'

As the prisoners moved away, she let her eyes settle on the luckless contingent now huddled as best they could in the shade. They were still shackled, still did not know what they were doing there without a future. The tears came again to my mother's eyes. She never saw these of our people again, or heard of their fate. The constabulary in Wyndham covered the actions well.

An arrangement had for a while been in place with Ah Kim to care for children like my mother, the unfortunate victims of the new policy of assimilation. His market garden and store on the road to the Halls Creek goldfields was ideally placed to hide them. As well as his own part-Chinese, part-Aboriginal children, there were others living nearby on the stony slopes.

Ah Kim saw the entourage coming. He stiffened, swallowed his dignity. Any words he considered saying to the man in uniform would have to wait for the appropriate time, if there was ever going to be one. He had always been concerned for the black women's bastard children. This new one was not the first—and she would not be the last.

'Who that, Lemon?' my mother heard the little girl with smooth brown skin ask her sister.

Lemon and her sister Orange had been playing under the paw-paw trees when they saw the sorry sight turn up in the heavy dust. They had been given the unusual nicknames according to their separate responsibilities in the shop. As was the custom, all the wares for sale were on display. Precious food items were most likely to somehow disappear, so Ah Kim placed his little girls to watch them, one behind the orange stall, and the other behind the lemons.

Now the little girls' eyes lit up. Coming towards them was another of their kind. The same age, the same skin colour. Someone else to play with.

'What's her name?' Orange asked.

'I dunno,' came Lemon's reply. 'Might be that policeman leave her here, too. She proper frighten' this one.'

They watched silently as their father patiently finished his work and placed the handmade kerosene tin watering can in its usual place. Straightening up, he untied his calico apron and looked at his visitors. 'Policeman bastard,' he muttered to himself.

He had seen this many times before but had not yet come to accept the savage act. He had no regrets ever since he left his Chinese homeland, but this still hurt him inwardly. The woman he called his wife was black, a Gajerong native of this country. They had two little girls, a boy and would have more to come. He loved them only as a father could and shuddered at the thought that, if he had not cared for them, they also would have been taken away.

Their curiosity aroused, the two girls ran to their father to get a closer look. They knew their mother would already be heading to the rear of the shack to hide in the foliage that the market gardens offered. She feared that perhaps some among the prisoners in the chained contingent across the creek would recognise her and report on her whereabouts. She still had to answer for breaking her cultural marriage protocol. Her promised man may still hold a grudge. Already, she knew, her immediate tribal family, who worked for Ah Kim and lived on the side of the hill a little distance away, would have slipped silently into the scrub as soon as they saw the small movement of dust approaching.

My mother stayed at Ah Kim's for several weeks. Her memory of two soft, brown-skin girls, their father the kind Chinese man, and their mother who would cry for her, lingered all her life.

Many times I have gone to this quiet, abandoned location with my own family, to sit in the extreme heat and stillness and defy the images of the past to reveal themselves. For it seems Ah Kim also had a mixed background. Much later, when he was old and illness threatened, he began to fear death in this unrelenting land. To satisfy his God when his departure finally came, he prepared his own grave. In his spare moments he constructed a pathway, straight up the hillside, some five hundred yards to a small level ridge. Here he dug a hole, appropriately placed, facing both the setting sun and his homeland. As he grew older and his illnesses slowly sapped his energies, he would painfully climb the pathway and sit beside his grave. On the day of his final sickness, he did not have the energy to climb the hill. He lay in his bed, only to be taken by a policeman to Wyndham where he died. The ruins of his market garden are still there, an epitaph to his struggle, and that of many others.

To the Mission

As for my mother, the missionaries at the Forrest River Aboriginal Mission had been informed by the police of her whereabouts. Arrangements needed to be made for her travel to the mission. Before long, my mother left Ah Kim's and was escorted into the bustling township of Wyndham where she disappeared forever from her Marlngin people.

A new era had begun for her. The boat came and took her away. The memories of the camels, the Afghans, the Aboriginal prisoners and white policeman were now completely obliterated by the swell and rush of that salty tidal estuary, the Cambridge Gulf. The huge expanse of dirty water heaved, dangerously tossing the small boat loaded with supplies.

My mother had already gone through unbearable torture and was now once more facing a cruel situation. No wonder she was bewildered. Where was her mother? She screamed as the small boat pounded its way across the rough waters. Her body felt battered, ragged. It seemed there was no purpose in her life. Why are they doing this? Why can't anyone hold me? Nobody cared, nobody saw her terror. Nobody told her why she had been so callously torn her away from her mother's loving arms.

She hid from the wind-tossed waters as much as she could under the tarpaulin covering the bags of oats. The bags were warm and offered a strange smell. Little did she know this was going to be her lot for the next twenty years, calico covering and porridge, darkness and ongoing terror. When would this shocking journey come to an end? She cried for her mother, for her brother, and she cried for herself.

Going Home

For years after having been snatched away, Mum grieved for her mother. Long after settling in Wyndham, she would still continuously approach Aboriginal stockmen droving cattle in from the Northern Territory. 'You know my mother?' she would ask. 'Mary, Mary Boonay? Spring Creek? Mistake Creek? Limbunya? Any way? That way? Got a brother too. His name is Ben, Ben Ogden. That's my name too, before I married him,' she'd say, glancing towards Dad.

Finally, word came through two men who had come droving on the stock routes. July Oakes and Bill Laurie, both relatives from my mother's people, broke the news. Mum wept.

'That old woman still alive, and she told us that she never stopped crying for you when they dragged you away, a long time ago. She still cried when we told her; you were here, living in Wyndham, with six kids and a good husband. Bunuba man, got one leg,' we told her. Cousin July went on with his welcome news: 'When you got taken, that old woman was no good, proper sick for long time. She ran away bush, take your brother Ben, and hide him with that desert mob blackfellas. Warlpiri mob, I think,' he told my still tearful mother.

'One old white man found him living with that mob in the desert and took him; look after him properly like his own son. His name is Matt Savage. Living in Alice Springs now, got three daughters. Funny thing, he's got a buggered-up leg, too. Never stop him from being a drover. Good bugger. Your brother Ben, working in Lewis Creek country now, outstation there somewhere.' The stories unfolded. 'He got a wife too, same name like your mother. Big boy for him there, too. Somewhere. First one. Ronnie, they call him.'

Bill Laurie had also made contact and invited us all to come to the Negri race meeting. 'That old woman will come on the station truck. They want you there. You got to go, might be last time, last chance to catch him up. Everything. He want you there!'

Mum was beside herself with the news. She cried for days, but after a while, all was in readiness: food, a drum of fuel, a drum of water and presents for Granny Mary Boonay. Our excitement grew as well. It was our first trip like this ever. A real holiday.

Early one morning, we left Wyndham. Jack Barnett, a contract fencer, had an old Bedford truck and he allowed Dad to borrow it. A journey of a lifetime was ahead of us. We drove towards the sunrise, past the Overflow Crossing on Parry's Creek where we broke down some years before, crossed the Ord River near Ivanhoe Station then through the treacherous Cockatoo Sands. After three days, we reached the Behn River.

'Not far now,' Dad said. 'We'll be there before sundown. Give us a chance to find the Mistake Creek Station mob's camp.'

By now, Mum only gave attention to our youngest, mostly busying herself with her preparations for the homecoming. Thirty years of silent, lonely tears she'd had, always wondering what if, why, when. All of this simply welled up in her quivering body as we shuddered over the black soil ridges in the old truck, in and out of stony creeks. She covered her wet eyes with a light towel. She could remember her mother as a young woman, her physical warmth and ever-comforting voice. There was no face in her memory, however. Time had erased it.

Harsh Memories

Although my mother was a mature woman, she had not fully prepared herself for what was going to happen to her now. The memories flooded back. Again, she could hear the gunshots of the early morning raid, the heart wrenching screams and wailing as the physical parting took place. The march into Wyndham on the mule and then the journey on the camel dray. Little Orange and Lemon. Where were the two little girls who shared everything with her, so many years ago, now? She knew their father, Ah Kim, had died but had never heard where they had been taken.

She relived the lonely, dark, sweltering nights locked in the girl's dormitory at Forrest River Mission. Smoke from a special wood collected during the day, warded off the millions of mosquitoes who preyed on the thin, shabbily dressed bodies all huddled together out of friendship, yearning and lost parental love. Most nights, the girls would chatter away, telling stories and sharing secrets. Laughing aloud, they'd provoke each other into all sorts of mischief until someone would call out, 'Hurricane lamp! Hurricane lamp! Father Gribble coming, you mob. Shut up! He gonna flog us.'

The staff and missionaries kept an eagle eye on the girls at Forrest River. 'Don't pretend you're sleeping, girls,' they would call out in response to the sound of feigned snoring. 'If I hear you one more time it's punishment for you—all in front of everybody, too. And don't forget to say your prayers to the Almighty. The Bishop is coming two weeks from now. His Grace will want to hear you recite those holy scriptures. Remember John 3:16.'

Mum had told us how all the girls brought in from all over the Kimberley and surrounds, planned and hoped for the day they would leave this dark dungeon. At night they would whisper to each other the secrets of their chosen loved one or the young man they hoped to marry, or even run away with into the bush. Most were patient and let their eyes do the talking. But alas, their champions were also under lock and key, and a good distance away. Love would have to wait a little longer.

Some young men were daring and broke into the girls' dormitory, using keys made from mouldings of soap that they had hastily pressed the original into. When Tenny (Tennyson) Thompson, the missionary assistant, was not watching they'd slip in. But Mum's boyfriend, now her husband driving this truck, was handicapped by having just one leg. Their courtship would have to be in the open.

As children, the girls at the mission were placed under strict ruling. As they grew up and learnt of their traditional marriage commitment, many of them went through a different type of torment. For some, this may have been a thankful release from the white man's detention as they bided their time. When the holiday bush excursions came, they could be whisked away by parents and elders for the necessary ceremonies. The lucky ones accepted the Indigenous culture for, rigorous as it was, it guaranteed survival of their people. The bastardisation happening before their eyes would prove to be totally devastating. Others were affected by the new blood of mixed Aboriginal youth now on site, each bringing a different version of life as it changed within the compound. Soon enough, the anguished memory of a black mother in a far off, unknown place would come to take second place to the challenge of survival. Pain and suffering, degradation and humiliation, many suffered under the devout teachings of the Church of England, where emphasis was placed on God, King and Country. Whose country?

'Look out for black Tom,' the girls threatened each other laughingly. 'He gonna sting you today, you talkin' like that. Sister hear you and old Tenny Thompson whip you!'

But one misdemeanour and out came the whipping stick (black Tom). It was a strict life. Their stomachs would rebel something awful against the diet of ground wheat or oats with dripping. The mission could never keep up the required food, even though they had their own supply from the fruit and vegetable gardens and complemented it with bush tucker from fishing and bush excursions.

New, younger girls from the far reaches of the Kimberley always found it difficult to adjust. Small groups developed to protect each other. My mother spoke proudly all her life of the powerful bonds that formed in the prison-like dormitory. Mum befriended a short, beautiful girl called Lily (later known as Lily Johnson). All of their moments of pain and happiness were shared and as a result, they called each other 'mate' right to the end of their lives. Her other close friends were equally pretty, and strong in mind. They had to be to survive. They all became my respected aunties forever. Sue, Ivy, May, Elsie, Molly, Eileen and Daphne. Some were direct relatives and as we grew, my mother taught us how to respect these persons so we would reap the benefits of traditional connections.

Under the cross of the Church of Saint Michael, the girls persevered, seeking respite although the way was not yet known to them. For some, the teachings of Jesus of Nazareth, Christ the Son of God, who they learnt to address as the Almighty, would be the only respite they would understand all of their lives. The spirituality of their own ancient culture was replaced by a relatively new religion. Christianity helped their lives along with beads, axes, food, clothes and lollies. And now a cross would take them to their graves.

Granny's Country

Mum was still thinking about these things by the time we reached the bustling picnic race meeting camping ground. All spread out along both sides of a large creek, it was easy to distinguish the

Aboriginal area. The low bushes and trees were colourful, with all sorts of clothing spread out and drying.

Dad drove slowly on the outskirts of the hundreds of camps. We children, eyes wide, cackled away noisily like apostle birds. Mum, her anxiety now high above all measure, searched the camps for signs. After many stops and inquiries, choking dust completely covering us all, Dad finally found out where we had to go.

'I think that's the camp,' he said quietly.

Mum was jolted into responsibility now, her mind racing again after her visit to her troubled past. There was much confusion. She sat uncomfortably in the truck, gazing at nothing in particular.

'Yes,' Dad unexpectedly interrupted her thoughts.' That's them, I think. Those old Aboriginal women sitting apart from everyone else across the steep creek, they are expecting us.'

He stopped the truck and warned all us kids to keep quiet and stay put. Then he clambered out of the truck to allow the yearning eyes across the tortured ground to confirm that he was indeed the one-legged husband of Mary Boonay's daughter, Polly.

The whole camp across the creek became hushed. Immediately, it was obvious who our maternal grandmother was. Trembling violently, a silver haired, tall, very old Aboriginal lady emerged from among the small group. As she arose, we heard the high-pitched wail from within her body. As one, the others gathered around her, crying softly. She began to strike her head with the sharp stone she carried to display her extreme sorrow and pain. There was blood on her glistening silver hair, oozing down her face, and soaking into her old dusty dress.

'Granny, oh Granny,' another strong voice exclaimed. 'Stop now old woman.' The other old lady was soothing her. Up until that moment, we had not understood a word of what was being said. 'She there now. That girl been come back. We go now, on other side.'

Still seated in the cab, my mother was unable to move. Dad walked to her side of the truck, gazed at her with glistening eyes and waited. Eventually she found some inner strength, moved out, immediately collapsing onto the dusty ground. Tearfully she gathered her composure, pulled herself up on her feet, wiped her face and surprisingly spoke in a clear dignified manner. 'I'll go myself, Guinea. All you kids, wait here.'

Sobbing and wailing loudly, the group of old Aboriginal women were already on the creek bed, slowly moving across the shingles and dried flood debris. As they saw Mum approaching, the years of agony, the unknown, came flooding up in the most heart-wrenching wail that I have ever heard and Mum was completely immersed among the women.

Together at Last

My mind was a blur. What was going on? The crying was beginning to torment me. Then the Aboriginal women all began to strike themselves with stones, and the blood began to flow again. Where was my mother? Surely they're hurting her. I screamed at Dad to go and help Mum but he ignored me. This enraged me something terrible. I did not know what came over me. I leapt off the truck and ran down towards the small group, overwhelmed by instincts I could not control. As I ran, I cried and called out to my mother, my father, my culture. Somewhere between the two groups I weakly stumbled to and fro, bewildered. I had not achieved anything. I did not know what I was doing. I was just responding to something beyond my capacity to understand at the time. Dad stumbled down the steep creek bank, took my hand and hauled my drained body back to the truck. My other brothers and sisters stared at me, all affected by our emotional experience, but mostly wondering what was I doing going off my brain like that. No one spoke. I sat apart from the rest, isolated in my thoughts.

After a long while Mum came back with Granny Mary Boonay. Together at last. After all those years of loneliness and yearning.

There were more tears now, but only tears of joy. I was afraid to meet my granny, thinking she might tell me how stupid I was. But there was no difference in the love she brought. Never did I see her let her daughter's hand go in all that time we were together.

Two days went by in a flash. The race meeting ended. We said solemn goodbyes with the promise we would return the next year.

But the Kimberley was a big country still, and it was difficult to organise or acquire transport without money or assistance. When Jack Barnett died a little later we had no more opportunities to go to the next race meeting. We did not see our grandmother ever again.

If it was intended that we share just two days of my grandmother's traditional cultural life, then I accept it. Her spiritual presence was profound, and the effect she had on my mother—and me—equally astonishing. Granny Boonay was clearly one of the most important influences in our lives, even though Mum had only known her mother for six years—and those two precious days.

Kindred Spirits

Kindred Spirits

History is uncanny, somehow kind in the way it brings kindred spirits together. From my youth, I had understood my mother's traditional cultural values, even though there were times when her Christian beliefs over-rode all else. For my part, there was a responsibility to recognise her people and their protocols of traditional marriage. I was curious, had a burning desire to test what was surging through me. I had a duty to find out for myself.

Before my commitment with Margaret, as a teenager I traveled the state of Western Australia, searching for the one person who, according to Mirriwoong culture, was my destiny, my appropriate marriage partner. Eventually I found her. It was not as hard as I expected. The Department of Native Welfare had dossiers on every person of Aboriginal descent.

She too was displaced, not attached to her culture, and lived in a different environment from the traditional one. Like me, her focus was survival. Our young lives had been so similar although we had never known each other. Distance and devastating circumstance had created enormous barriers.

I came home alone, confused, and somewhat in despair, having experienced a shattering rejection of our culture by the so-called modern world. There was no doubt in my mind that the person I had met and spoken to was kind and understood my integrity. There was no need for words, only a solemn farewell and a guarantee of a lifelong Mirriwoong friendship. Now many years have gone by, but the trust and friendship are still in place.

When my relationship with Margaret began, her soul proved to be compatible with my ailing spirit. She was no stranger to heartbreak, torment, and isolation. As a child, she had been abandoned by her mother, a single parent, who had suffered immensely under the Native Welfare regime and the onslaught of the pastoral era in the Kimberley early last century.

Margaret appeared instantly to understand my endless quest for some answers to our mixed up cultural dilemmas. However, her vagabond history had given her the title of bastard early in her life. I was shocked to discover that these things mattered, and somewhat hurt when it was rumoured that our traditional backgrounds were too disparate for us to marry. She was considered a person of no consequence and thus was not seen as being an appropriate marriage partner for me. (The very fact that my parents had legally married in a church had a significant bearing on our standing among many in both the white and black communities in those days.)

Nevertheless we persevered; we were not to be deterred. How could this enchanting person before me be guilty of carrying a stigma of breeding and colour? Perhaps out of guilt and self-blame, Margaret would talk to me for hours, telling of her childhood. As we sat in our chosen places, or sometimes just walking on our hallowed ground, the Gully marsh, I listened in wonder to the circumstances in her life as an unwanted girl-child. How lucky I was to be under the protection of Polly and Cyprian Birch and also to have their name.

Margaret's earliest memories always took her to Moola Bulla. It was known as the 'Gov'ment Place'. People of mixed Aboriginal heritage were dumped there and a forced process of assimilation of Indigenous people began. Many young families lived there in army-type, steel framed and tin roofed huts. Their existence was based on what was produced on the cattle station and anything else they could find to eat.

Margaret's mother lived here with her little daughter. They were lucky in the sense that there were many Gidja people present so the business of sharing and caring for each other actively helped their survival.

She remembers going to school for the first time. The class was all Aboriginal, standard wooden desks on a dirt floor under a bush timber and spinifex grass cover. Mrs Gill, the European teacher, devotedly taught the rowdy bunch. In the front near the black board was a picture of a future king of Australia. A youthful Charles, Prince of Wales, smiled daily at his constituency.

Margaret only slept with her mother. During the day her activities were with the other children. In small groups away from school and other responsibilities, they searched always for extra food. Everything it seemed was government supplied. Rations were limited. There was no choice in clothing or anything else for that matter. It was cold in winter and all the children suffered from hideous, red-raw, painful chilblains, nasty gurgling coughs, and continually running noses.

Raggedly dressed, they presented themselves, one day no

different than the rest. Everything was a laugh, a part of growing up with the rest, girls, and boys together. But there were the dreaded moments when some depraved man who she had previously trusted, accosted her. Even at a young age, the alarm bells rang and Margaret learnt to watch for the signs. No one warned her but the little girl quickly built up a defence mechanism, never knowing when to sleep safely and never quite sure where to place her trust.

Moola Bulla Native Settlement had hundreds of goats for food and milk supply. Habit brought the goats back into the open yards late in the afternoon for the night's sleep. This was the cue for the vagabond children to sneak into the yard, identify the friendly nanny goats with bulging udders of milk, and help themselves. If they did not have cups or billycans they drank straight from the teats, squeezing with grubby little hands. They could not understand when adults told them to stay away from the goat yard, for fear of physical punishment from their Native Welfare minder. But their little bodies always stunk because to get the milk they had to lie on the ground in inches of wet and dry goat dung—a dead giveaway!

Life for the young Margaret Bridge was not much different to anyone else's on the settlement. She understood clearly what was happening to her people. A dreadful thought. The shame carried by Aboriginal women who had fraternised with whitefellas was long-lasting.

By 1955 Moola Bulla had reached its use by date. Perhaps the government of the time, under some political pressure, had called it a day for this type of institution. In any case, for reasons unknown to Margaret, and indeed the whole Aboriginal population of Moola

Bulla, the government gave up the East Kimberley Aboriginal Reserve. It became a pastoral property and was leased by an enterprising millionaire called Goldman. Unfortunately, however, his interests did not at all lay in caring for hundreds of destitute Aboriginal people.

As a result, all the Aboriginal people there were virtually evicted. Within one day they were forced to leave for Halls Creek or elsewhere. There was no food on arrival, no home to move into. The government had washed its hands of its responsibility and completely turned its back. Dumped along the creek bed were other Aboriginal fringe dwellers in the Halls Creek area; this is where many of these refugees headed. It was just as well Aboriginal people were linked by tribal connections and cared for each other.

Their plight was of no concern for Goldman once he had bought his pastoral rights. He was sensible enough to keep the skilled workers but still paid with rations. The rest faced a life-time of nothingness, of endless torture, tears and misery. All at the stroke of a pen.

Margaret's mother was forced to seek employment and eventually landed a domestic help job at the hotel in the old township of Halls Creek which had sprung up as a result of the discovery of alluvial gold in the magnificent ridges. The proprietors were Robert and Beryl Shaw-Moody who, as time passed by, abandoned the mud brick building, and re-established the Kimberley Hotel in the new town. Although Halls Creek was a perfect setting there was no room for expansion, let alone an influx of Aboriginals.

Quite clearly, Margaret remembers sitting in an insignificant corner in the old hotel. Her mother laboured there for a pittance, making sure she snaffled enough leftovers for her somewhat derelict offspring. There were always scrapings off the dinner plates and as soon as her duties were done, she presented her mouth-watering gifts. Depending on the day's turn of events, they would sit together, sometimes solemn and quiet, their shared yearnings bringing them momentarily close. Eye contact, a little game of touch and giggle, the mother would tenderly wipe the corners of little Margaret's eyes and then with finger and thumb, ever so gently, clinch the nostrils and draw out the ever present ooze from the little girl's nose.

Mrs Shaw-Moody was quite an elaborate lady, as Margaret recalls. She held herself in high esteem and adorned herself with luxurious clothing, jewellery, painted red nails, red lips and high-heeled shoes that matched the colour of her frock of the day. She surrounded herself with tiny dogs of the poodle variety, and was prone to dressing them up in ribbons and bows; they were her real accessories.

Margaret soon found herself being dressed like the poodles by Mrs Shaw-Moody. This was indeed a shock. At Moola Bulla she was used to wearing second-hand clothing and flour bag dresses. Now it was party dresses with all the trimmings. At the time it was such a good feeling for a little girl, but now she shudders at the thought of such hypocrisy.

There were not many European children in Halls Creek but the telegraph linesman, John Gilfoyle, had a son who received correspondence lessons. So the boy, the same age as Margaret, shared these lessons with her for a short while.

Soon after, her mother chose to move on. She went to another employment in the developing new town of Halls Creek. Things started to go from bad to worse from this point on. After a short while she did not like the life in town and decided to move on again.

Margaret's mother told her that her grandmother should be in the Mabel Downs Station area. Her name was Ruby Gilinjil, and she was a traditional person. Also, her Aunt Ivy Rademe (Ivy Mills) was known to be in Wyndham with her husband and a young family. A family reunion would have been a magnificent morale booster, but unfortunately it was not to be.

On arriving at Mabel Downs there was no knowledge of her grandmother's whereabouts, however a new and sudden set of circumstances changed her life forever. Margaret sadly remembers the heartbreak when told she would be taken back to Halls Creek. Her mother had met a man and they planned to pursue a life of their own. It really sunk in when she watched her mother leave.

Eventually her mother married this man and raised another family. Margaret does not blame her mother for the dire life she led, but she does openly regret the loss of parental love and care. In times of profound illness, there was no one to hold and comfort her. She developed rheumatic fever at an early age and as a result suffered poor health throughout her life. The conditions in the sometimes squalid situations she lived in took their toll.

Margaret was left with other relatives, Biddy and Jack Trust. Up until that time, there had only been the two of them. It left a huge void. Questions crept into her mind. Why was she being abandoned? Was she not loved? Did not anyone care? Who would want her now, she wondered, was there anyone at all?

Biddy and Jack, having a small family of their own, accepted Margaret as their own. It proved to be difficult at first to replace the hurt felt by the small, broken, shattered child with new confidence. But eventually she responded to the Aboriginal love and care that had been missing in her life up until now. She tells me, time and time again, that she will never, ever forget them.

Having suddenly realised that her mother may never return, she felt she would somehow have to deal with her yearnings and grief privately. But Biddy and Jack, without neglecting at all the needs of their own demanding brood, made space and gave love to Margaret as well.

Together they reconstructed her shattered life, restored her confidence. Margaret was only nine years old and learning fast. She responded brilliantly and retains to this very day the aura so lovingly passed on to her from those delightful carriers of Aboriginal dignity and spirituality.

Biddy and Jack Trust were associated with the United Aborigines Mission based in Halls Creek. As a result of being evicted from Moola Bulla, they too had been looking for an alternate way of life. As the assimilation process took over and reduced access to traditional Aboriginal land was recognised, Aboriginal values were reduced.

There was little movement among our Aboriginal people now. Only males having the ability to seek work on cattle stations traversed the Kimberley, making the long droving trips to the Wyndham Meatworks.

It became obvious at this time that the gospel of Jesus Christ was having a profound effect on the Aboriginal people. So vulnerable in their present state of mind with virtually no choice in life whatsoever, this religion offered comfort to the greater majority of our kinfolk across the Kimberley hinterland. Again, if Margaret had not already learned of another spiritual way, she may not have survived.

Coming of age, Margaret was sent to the township of Derby, in the West Kimberley to live in the newly established United

Aborigines Mission Hostel. Here she was required to attend high school. Religious studies were compulsory and part of the association with the United Aborigines Mission Hostel. Again, she became aware of isolation, loneliness, and the need for Aboriginal family connections. Very little was on offer. As a lonely teenage girl, without support, money, or family, she again became vulnerable and sought any way out. After working for the Native Welfare Department for a short term, she moved to Wyndham to live with her mother and her new family. Ten years had passed since she'd last seen her mother; she was not yet seventeen.

They say that country boys are slow as a wet week. When Margaret came to Wyndham she lived next door to our family, in a tin shed down the old Gully. By this time, I had given up all hope of finding a wife anywhere between here and the black stump.

Perhaps the fault was my own. Who would want to marry someone who ran everywhere he went, through the town and surrounding bush, carried several spears when hunting, and still lived with his parents? But Margaret, goodness knows how, saw some potential in me. In two years, we planned our destiny together, all the time walking on hallowed ground, the Gully area, and the land of our spirits. From that one fine morning in September 1964 my life changed forever, although the road to our marriage vows was troubled with many cultural barriers.

There would be no turning away from any looming issue that was difficult. Already, Margaret's capability and spiritual control was enormous. She soon became the dynamic driving force that had just about everything to do with what we both are today.

Margie's and my realisation that our spirits had been broken for some time, and that we had been living according to other people's principles, made us more adamant that we should use our new-found sense of freedom to create a small part of the world in the way we dreamed. Our own Dreaming, as it were. The spirits would never leave or betray us.

Then I had a dreadful industrial accident that left me broken in spirit for a while, and disabled for the rest of my life. I remember the incident clearly, as it changed my life forever.

I was working on the waterfront at Wyndham—it was extremely difficult manual labour. Many state and foreign ships came in on a regular basis in the cooler months. With a team of workmen our job was to load and unload the cargo, working from eight to fourteen hours each day, sometimes seven days a week. Most of our work crew were capable and experienced enough to endure the hardships of the job.

When ships came from the United Kingdom for the loading of frozen meat from the meatworks, the system changed. This was fast-moving cargo. Rakes of trucked meat (six to a rake) were brought down along the three-foot, six-inch gauge railway line from the freezers at the meatworks, as fast as the old diesel engine train dared to go. A single track led to the wharf, which then divided into three tracks to allow shunting and maneuvering of trucks.

I somehow always ended up with the job of being train guard or shunter on the fast-moving engine. This train rarely stopped for a break, constantly moving from pick-up point to loading zone, sometimes supplying cargo to two holds of a ship at once. I was strong and fit and could run all day, carrying out the shunting work as required. The working period for the loading of meat boats was 7:30am to 9:30pm (in twelve hour periods) each day. This could go on for weeks at a time.

This particular day, 1 September 1964, I was on the front truck that was being pushed by the engine at break-neck speed on the single track towards the wharf. There were two ships in the harbour, two trains working the system, scores of men relying on a hazard-free work place. Another shunter had the responsibility of throwing the points (cheese knobs) to allow an engine to move from one track to another, on this occasion to allow clear passage for our engine to pass. This was done but it seems that a serious malfunction occurred. As we hurtled down the tracks and crossed the railway line points, I felt the truck I was on, lift off the line.

Immediately I threw up my arms to signal the driver to stop, then turned and looked back. I was shocked to see all of the trucks bucking as if they were going over a huge speed bump. Each truck contained two cargo nets loaded with twenty-eight pound cartons of frozen meat. Almost instantly the truck I was riding on began to tip dangerously. I knew it was not going to be possible to stick with the train and ride it out—the train was coming apart quickly.

My options were limited. There was a long shed two metres away to my left, loaded railway trucks on my right—I would be mangled if I jumped in either direction. Only two options, then. Wait until we had passed the shed and train and jump into the Cambridge Gulf, about forty feet below—but then the trucks could follow and land on top of me. My mind was made up— jump off and out-run the jumbled wreckage. It began to slow and roll over, spewing out cartons in all directions like missiles; I was hit several times as I waited for my moment to jump clear. It came: I jumped, my life flashed before my eyes and death stared me in the face.

I landed with great force on the wooden decking and railway lines. My left leg went into a crevice and out again, there was a tug on my limb as I went rolling over and over. Cartons were raining and flying in all directions amid the torturous screaming of twisting metal and the dull thud of the timbers as the railway trucks were torn apart.

The whole assembly, a hundred tons or more of death landed around me. I wanted to get up and run but couldn't. What was stopping me? One quick step and over I would go, my leg must be broken! Never mind! Keep going. Keep going till the noise stops. There was no pain, only a desire to get away from there and live. I stumbled, jumped, rolled, kept going, running, feeling a severe jarring on my left knee. The din ceased, everything went quiet. I stopped my urgent activity and collapsed to the deck.

To my horror, I saw my left foot, still in the boot, stretched at an obscene angle back toward my kneecap. There were blood-covered sinews and tendons and some skin still attached but hanging out the top of my socks. Aghast, I realised that I had run some fifty metres on the stump of the bones in my leg—the foot had been ripped off by the crevice when I first landed. I quickly positioned my foot where it could receive the benefit of the spurting blood from my leg. I was alive, that's all that mattered to me then. I looked into the morning sun, and thought, 'Yes, I will see another one.'

Suddenly I was lifted by three men. Another man, Frank Chulung walked alongside and carried my bloodied, almost severed foot. I assessed my plight and thought, 'Two snips with a pair of scissors and my foot's gone.' Why should I grumble, my dad had lost almost a whole leg when he was thirteen, so I had better not complain to him. All he would say, I'm sure, is, 'You alright, boy.' My wedding would have to be postponed. Arrh well!

Somehow the Wyndham doctors, Tony House and his wife Jill, managed to extricate my foot from the boot, unravel the mess and position my foot in a more appropriate place—at the end of my leg. Another operation later on had steel pins locking the joints together, thus disabling me for the rest of my life. I was fast becoming the image of my father, in more ways than I could possibly have imagined.

In 1966 I received an offer of compensation for the serious injury that resulted in a 42% disability forever in my left leg. I was reluctant to accept anything as I was concerned about future complications and developments in technology that may improve my situation. My union representative advised me that future developments should not be expected, so I reluctantly accepted a little over $1800.

Wonder what I would have got for 43%? But there again, I was not yet a citizen of this country.

Margie and I had planned to marry on 30 November 1964. We eventually married in 1965. Like my father, I stood before my bride with only one boot—the other was draped in a full-length plaster cast. People noticed but politely declined to comment.

All Still Here

All Still Here

The Old Fella

I think back through the years
As a boy in my old home
How my life was filled with wondering
What would happen in time to come
Dad said one day you'll be a man
With my name to guard and live
Things will be much better then
You've just got to learn to give

I reckoned he knew what he talked about
As he lived and showed me life
I depended on him for everything
And how to face our living strife
Heartache, misery and prejudice
Were problems he took in stride
Singing, sporting and happiness
You'd always have Dad on side

I was proud one day to call him
Say old fella can we talk?
I have found myself a young woman
It's time for me to get up and walk
He did not answer but smiled
Man to man our vibrations flowed
He was satisfied with my decisions
I was glad his contentment showed

He was soon to leave us
I know not why the plan
Perhaps the Spirit in his reckoning
Knows what's best for his own
I mourned his loss with bitterness
For things I never yet learned
Why should he go and leave us
Still unaccustomed and spurned

Miracles occur within us
Those of us who think we are meek
The blood and customs of our fathers
Bring strength to those who seek
I know now the reasons for his action
My Dad, the teacher, the man
I am just another of his image
That my sons in seeking can learn.

I have chosen not to leave the area of the Kimberley my parents came to call home during the years of World War II. In fact, Wyndham has become the home to all the generations of the Birch family since Cyprian and Polly began their search for kindred country and a peaceful existence. It may be unusual these days, but my siblings—Rosemary, Laurie, Helen, Ted, Charlie—and I all live close to where we grew up in and around the Gully.

The traditional Aboriginal people of this area have been kind to us. We have learned to understand their culture and language, and in return we have respected the benefits of this awareness. We have learned to use the Aboriginal way to express and interpret every feeling and experience which has enabled us to survive in this land in the early years of yet another century.

Rosemary, my oldest sister, was born in 1936. She was our keeper, protector and unofficial advisor outside home early in our lives.

Intelligent, she progressed quickly. Nothing, it seemed, was too hard for her. Leaving school, and with an added advantage of a Perth-based education, she worked in the secretarial and administrative sections of the Department of Native Welfare. Later she took up nursing positions in Perth and also back at Wyndham.

She married Kurt Adolf Beck, a German migrant, and then began a family home in the Kimberley. They eventually moved to Melbourne, back to the Kimberley, to Goa in India where she stayed for two years, before moving through European countries on their way to Germany for another two years. Her husband was a riverboat captain with stevedoring experience. Hence their lifestyle was hectic, living on huge river barges, delivering cargo along the River Rhine.

By this time she had three children and her old yearnings for the bush in the Kimberley had set in again. The family divided; she came home with a son and a daughter, the other son still lives in Germany but is not there by choice. Born in Germany and a citizen of that country, when he came for a visit, his Australian visa only allowed a twelve month stay.

Rosemary has three grandchildren and ten great-grandchildren. She is now retired in the Kimberley, her home.

Lawrence Ashton (Laurie), my older brother, was born in 1939. He became my companion and advisor but generally did what he pleased. His life, too, was filled with heartache and misery, plenty of action and high drama; it warrants a story of its own.

After leaving school in 1953, his first serious employment was with the Native Welfare Department as an assistant. I remember being with him on his training exploits, learning to type on an ancient cumbersome typewriter, in the old Wyndham post office. His job with Bill Andrews, the Native Welfare Officer, kept him busy dealing with Aboriginal issues from that era. The welfare officers made annual visits to all stations in the East Kimberley, keeping a dossier on the Aboriginal population, maintaining statistics and general information about activities.

In 1959, Laurie married June Russ, daughter of a famous Kimberley pioneer, Fred Russ, who had developed two cattle properties, Gibb River and Mount Barnett. Years later, the pastoral market took a downturn, long before the tourism industry began to offer any respite. Poor future economics in the region forced Laurie and his family to sell up and commence a refrigeration repair business in Derby.

Laurie and June have three sons and five grandchildren, and live in semi-retirement back at Wyndham.

Helen Rose was born in 1942, a strong-willed individual. With early employment in the domestic area, she eventually married Robert Dryden (now deceased) and had seven children, twenty-two grandchildren and two great-grandchildren. She has lived in Perth, extensively in the Northern Territory and now is back home in the Kimberley.

Career-minded and conscious of the low economy in our region, she is mindful of the benefits of training. For a while, she was employed as an administrative assistant for Balangarr Aboriginal Corporation, an organisation that dealt with issues of a local Kimberley group of traditional landowners.

Edward William (Ted) was born down at the Six Mile Creek in Wyndham in 1944. Ted was unfortunate with his health in his early life and suffered immensely. However, he was made of stern stuff and I watched him grow to manhood, developing a magnificent, powerful body.

He married Dora Johnson from Halls Creek, the daughter of our mother's school mate Lily. They set up a home in Wyndham and raised a family. Having left school at the age of twelve for health reasons, Ted, like most of us, really had no skills to support a growing family. Undeterred, he flung himself into all sorts

211

of work, maintaining a dignity that kept him employable to the time of this writing.

Although all of us had the tendency to develop skills as we matured, and all of us inherited the ability to communicate, Ted went one better. He became a lay preacher. Currently, he is the resident pastor at the People's Church at Wyndham. He officiates at all ceremonies, burials and weddings and performs all the activities required of him in this particular calling. Being a licensed marriage celebrant, Ted performs these duties in surprising places and locations all over the East Kimberley.

Ted and Dora have four children and five grandchildren. They live a busy life, full of commitment to the community.

Leonard Charles (Charlie), the youngest in our family, was born in Wyndham in 1950. In the Gully, life was good for him. He had the advantage of a better education at the high school in Derby in the West Kimberley. With his birthright came a massive body frame, a Kimberley 'knock about' experience, a keen sense of humour and a strong capacity to impress and mingle with all manner of persons.

He was gifted with the ability to be comfortable among women and retain his manly physique. He became a tough bare-knuckle fighter, a hard working and industrious cattleman, station manager, rodeo rider, bull catcher, heavy machine operator, traveler of renown, not knowing where the sun was going to set on him next—a real Kimberley identity.

Somewhere in between his exploits he married Jane Russ, another daughter of the Kimberley pioneer Fred Russ. They had one son and two daughters and subsequently have grandchildren as well.

Leonard has not changed his lifestyle one bit and, I guess, the Kimberley expects that he should not.

Many things have taken the members of our family away from Wyndham—and each other—over the years. And our lives well and truly have had separate paths. But we've all come back to Wyndham eventually. It's a place where there is plenty of room for all our different callings. And there is space to look at each other with all of our many differences. Which is very fortunate, since we're all still here!

Yella Fella Dreaming

Yella Fella Dreaming

Dreaming

I ask the old ones of my Dreamtime
Their secret guarded for years
Show us to know the old homeland
Show us what is truly ours
With wisdom still from Dreamtime past
Folks pass the stories true
Who will listen? Who will tell?
Those who heed the heart are few

What we seek still surrounds us
Now painted different though
Look long and deep but find yourself
Before our old ones go
Times are quickly changing
Young eyes no longer see
The beauty of Dreamtime union
Of the land with you and me

Big country, big water, big Dreaming
Could be a thing of the past
Speak now old ones I beg of you
While you still have breath to last
For the love of our country
Show me your spirit concealed
That I may continue forever
A son of the Dreamtime revealed

I seek the Joys my father knew
I seek the Peace my mother sang
Dreamtime Spirit still holds you
Listen to their song.

There is always the yearning to find your traditional country and your place in this society. However, in the Kimberley, where our kin survive today, there is a fear that attitudes and expectations may differ, causing conflict in our families. Nonetheless, it is our belief that respect must be shown to our home country and our elders.

The Dreaming still exists, but these days the participants are from our present generations. Some of us are culturally gifted; others respond to another authority. We each have our individual callings.

As the township waxes and wanes with its various industries, the people who occupy the space come and go. Records are kept by those given that responsibility—but every one of us has memories.

Meanwhile, the south-east wind continues to soften the pressure on the minds of those who call Wyndham home. The change in the weather continues to nudge us. Do we respond? Can we respond?

My work has kept me close to our people. In my day I've been a team leader, ganger, leading hand, manager, union delegate, speaker and organiser. Having developed some leadership qualities from goodness knows where, by the mid-1970s I had worked my way into political positions. I was always coming out as a spokesperson.

I began to represent our Aboriginal people at the local, state, national and international levels. Over the years I have occupied a number of positions: National Aboriginal Conference (NAC) member for the Kimberley; South Pacific member for the World Council of Indigenous Peoples; Chairperson of the Executive Committee for the Kimberley Land Council (KLC); national member for the Council of Aboriginal Development (CAD); national member, Federation of Land Councils; Commissioner, Aboriginal and Torres Strait Island Commission (ATSIC); founding Chairperson, Joorook Ngarni Aboriginal Corporation; founding Chairperson, Wunan Regional Council (ATSIC); member, Wunan Regional Council (ATSIC); WA Chairperson, State Advisory Council (ATSIC); member of the Aboriginal Housing Board, Aboriginal Lands Trust, Aboriginal Legal Service, Kimberley Aboriginal Tourist Association and many others.

I have met some incredible people in my work and travels, and it has been my privilege to rub shoulders with many Aboriginal leaders and other dignitaries in Australia in the past twenty-five years. In far-off countries such as the United Kingdom, Canada, Switzerland, the United States of America and New Zealand, I have come across leaders who promoted Indigenous causes in a dignified and professional manner. Sometimes I forgot that I carried the same responsibility for my own people back in Australia. Alone in my hotel room I could not believe that, coming from such humble beginnings as an Aboriginal reserve on the outskirts of Wyndham, I had actually been given this task myself. Always, I still felt like the wide-eyed little boy from the Gully.

Many times when I was far away from the Kimberley, working at one thing or another, I would hear the singsong of the little silver eye bird down the creek in the mangroves near the Wyndham jetty. I'd see the bright little red and black crabs clicking away in the dark mud as they risked feeding away from their tube-like holes.

The educational options for me and my siblings were minimal at Wyndham Primary School. After reaching Grade Six we accepted a two-year correspondence course instead of traveling somewhere else for higher learning. Our parents had no money for boarding school, which in any case was only offered to the eldest in every family.

I escaped with my life after my accident on the Wyndham wharf, the very place where I grew up, but was left with a disability that hindered my physical capabilities for all my remaining years. Previously I had enjoyed a healthy life, physically fit beyond average. Now, I was just grateful for being alive. But this was a time of spiritual learning for me too.

I like to think that my early learning has stood me in good stead. Some things came easily, as I realised with time.

My years of public life coincided with major events of Indigenous importance, many taking place at the top level. I was completely staggered with the input required and gave everything that my Kimberley nurturing could allow me to give. There was a lot that I did not know and it took an effort to learn to carry myself with dignity and conduct myself as expected, in those duties.

I was among my own kind, working for our people in this vast expanse of Australia. In the depths of our political misery we, as the elected arm of Indigenous leadership, found a kindred spirit and wept together.

Sometimes the boardroom, with all its modern technology and conveniences, became transformed into a place of isolation. Sometimes it felt like a sacred place. As each person spoke, every-one in the room could feel the murmur of the Great Spirit. It moved across the sky. For some, its sound was of the sea, a roar, with purpose. For others, it was as if the very earth was tearing apart, trembling, as the great snake moved across the continent.

Not all of us, as we grappled with this new experience, under-stood it. Some promised to question their elders on return to the homelands. Always, there was the demand from our people to be fine-tuned, honed like a spearhead straight from the grinding stone.

We had been chosen as ambassadors to represent our people from all walks of life in Australia. Having formed a solid, united body (ATSIC), we then had to face the responsibility of develop-ing policies and implementing active programs which, within strict time-frames and limited budget constraints, would answer the needs of our people.

Sometimes we failed in the execution of our tasks. Other times, like seedlings responding to the sun, we were rejuvenated through meeting elders from the many reaches of this land. There were occasions when, like fish fighting the turbulence to achieve the final goal, we relentlessly persevered.

In the early years there were protest marches in capital cities, always the police contact, bruising from the masses in the crowd, loud shouting, the din, roaring in your ears. I'd look up to the sun and wonder if I would make it home this time.

When the doors of the old Parliament House in Canberra gave way under human force, people streamed past, screaming and yelling. Not part of the plan. Somebody fell down. Older persons had overestimated their capability. Euro-Australians were looking on bewildered, some not displaying any emotion, others showing clear disgust. Straightaway you could tell what their thoughts were.

Even through all of this my thoughts still would fly. Wyndham, where are you? Let me just be there, again, if I survive the tests of this world.

As they say, times were tough, but I do not know if this is entirely true. If you understood what was required, if you listened to the hidden spirit and obeyed, then there was no need to fear.

Several times over the years I was invited to functions: the residence of various Governors General, the inner sanctuary of Parliament House, the list goes on. We Indigenous representatives would arrive and, after the usual protocol, everyone mingled at leisure. Here were the stalwarts of Australian bureaucracy, commerce, industry, and politics. It always seemed to me that they appeared to be thoroughly enjoying themselves; they were merely jousting with the fractured Aboriginal assembly. Regardless of dress codes, we still appeared as a rabble. And if we thought we passed as acceptable, then more often than not our conversation skills let us down. These days, I am of the opinion that we were, in actual fact, lambs being prepared for the slaughter.

We all concentrated on the tasks ahead, and would try not to gather in defensive little packs talking of home, longing to be down by the creek, or whispering about the superb service that the parliamentary staff continually provided for us. We were expected not to engage in conversation with the staff.

I learned quickly that the average politician was expert in his or her field and it did not pay to mix with them or try to teach them something new about Aboriginal people. They knew all about us. There was an answer for everything.

Instead I chose, when speaking to these leaders of our nation, to inquire about personal issues, hobbies, of home and family, attitudes, and general interests. This way, I was able to communicate at my own pace and, at the same time, find out about the person. The policies they represented could be found in piles of volumes and read at a more convenient time. But the usual line at events was that they would remain tight-lipped, avoid the difficult issues, and call the function a cultural success.

Even though we met on a regular basis for ATSIC meetings, these parliamentary diversions seemed to add no momentum; they did not seem to contribute any political benefits at all. Most times, however, at these glorious events, there would be a magnificent four-stringed quartet. That I could really relate to! I'd just switch off and let the music linger in the air. The melody would spiritually draw me away, to my other world. It was so easy. I'd go back to my humble origins, forced once again to journey into my mind, but with my eyes open.

It would seem that I had not left Wyndham. My childhood tribulations were identical to what lay ahead. In my path there were such difficulties that somehow it seemed that things had not changed at all. I was still struggling on the shit cart.

Now that I have, to a degree, fulfilled most of life's options and ambitions as they presented themselves to me, I have come to the conclusion that the place you commence your journey must be where it ends. You must complete the full circle, so to speak. Far-off places are only illusions, dreams, as it were. My visions were on Wyndham all the time.

I believe it was my destiny to be born in this era, in this place, in this time. I have a responsibility by birthright. But I have had to find my way, struggle for my public achievements; they have not been a gift.

I am ever so grateful. Everything I ever needed was here in Wyndham. The world came to me. Often I have wondered if it was coincidence that my father came from the West Kimberley, and my mother from an area adjacent to the Northern Territory in the east. It was a union of Kimberley people that in the long run would immensely assist my political career—and help ease the tensions that have always existed among the Kimberley's many tribes.

When I was a small boy, my mother would bathe each one of us children in this huge galvanised tub. It was more than a bogey, it was a ritual. She would sing to us individually, each in turn. A moment of love, some space to breathe, covered in a blanket of parental care and affection. By the spirits of our ancestors, I was lucky.

With pride, I have passed on the ability to sing to my children, and they to theirs. But the greater majority of Indigenous people in this continent have been denied the right to pass on our traditional culture in this manner. Even so, wherever I journey in this vast country, I am pleased to see Indigenous folk still finding the time to communicate with the young, one way or another.

In the early days of European settlement in the Kimberley, little respect was shown for the inhabitants of this beautiful land. They had divided it equally among the many peoples and all worshipped the very ground they trod on. Our spirit, our Dreaming had been in place for thousands of years before the whitefella came with other intentions for the place.

Earlier in my unsettled life, I traveled Australia-wide, searching for goodness knows what, perhaps trying to fathom what lay in store for all of us. Tiring quickly of this land of the 'weird mob', I came home to take off my boots and to again straighten my spears. I was penniless and thin after spending my last pound in Queensland. It was a long road home—but a country boy never starves in the bush. Besides, I carried a guitar, my passport for every meal. Only Mum and Dad greeted me on return. I was not yet twenty-one.

I believe the attitudes of people of the Gully in Wyndham where I grew up were far more responsible for moulding my character than anything else. In the Gully I was exposed to every which way, every bloody Tom, Dick, Harry and Mary.

My first steps were in a Dreaming place not of my making. But like the wind, I have been constantly moving through the seasons; sometimes with just a murmur, then a flurry of gusts; sometimes a whirlwind, then a gentle sigh. It seemed I had a responsibility to create a buffer zone to protect the Dreaming as I understood it. This was my calling. No one has told me otherwise. In fact, I was encouraged in this pursuit by traditional elders from many Kimberley tribes.

I am humble with gratitude for my years that now exceed three score. My family is a great source of comfort, since my duties and responsibilities often seem to me to be enormous. Yet clearly, I have a purpose that has been there all the time.

My marriage has been my main strength. Margaret and I were rewarded with four children. Robyn Veronica was our first-born, and then came Wendy May, David Edgar and Simon Alfred. We now have, as well, two sons-in-law, one daughter-in-law, seven granddaughters and one grandson.

Somehow all my family has understood the need for survival. We are still together. Just as in my childhood, we huddle together for warmth, ask the older ones for wisdom, and cry together when it's needed.

There are many families in Wyndham like us. Stolen generations, the unwanted of this country. Yet here we all are at last, finding comfort in a lingering presence that perhaps some have not yet recognised. It's something worth fighting for.

I have learned from the traditional owners that the country around the Wyndham area is linked to one particular family, and in most areas, there is a buffer zone for neighbouring tribes. The East Kimberley has an abundance of bush tucker; parts of it are neutral space for our people to pass through for ceremonies and special gatherings. Unfortunately, these tracts have been dealt a cruel blow. Many in this country have no idea of the conse-quences of their actions and policies—and if they do, as they say at times, then they clearly show no concern.

Somehow we have to translate the variations in the land that lies before us, untangle the mess of what used to be our blood-lines, work out our priorities in a life where nothing is planned. Where are we to go? The only answer that appears on the horizon is to stay close, attached to our land or any land we are associated with. This, it seems to me, is the only way to retain our Aboriginal identity.

In Wyndham, a busload of tourists stops close by the big crocodile. Tired looking, they all drag themselves out, cameras ready. I watch as they fan out, chattering away. 'Look, Margie,' I say in astonishment, 'doesn't that old lady look like Mrs Flinders? And that old bloke over there with the walking stick, he looks a bit like old Jock Bentley.'

The faces of the past return again, in another time, another form, another spirit, to momentarily occupy this place. Maybe it is only my memory playing havoc, resisting the taunts of the modern world, even in Wyndham.

The earth gets on with its ritual, seasons come and go, the migration of people continues. One time, only the tribes of the region treaded the ground softly, solemn in their approach to the welcoming, rugged Warriu (Bastion Range). Perhaps tomorrow, they will meet with the Mirriwoong, or the Woolaja, or with others of their own kind.

Today, in Wyndham, all manner of mankind pass through. From under a shady tree, I sit with my family and observe them as they pass by.

Our daily rituals now take us to the supermarket—not so super, but it does the job. We go to the post office and bank agency. Most days, if there is a gentle breeze, you will find gatherings of Aboriginal folk in town, their eyes searching for a not so distant gratification, something to appease their unspoken spiritual but mostly physical desires.

Sometimes as I scan the jumbled mass of humanity, a faint aroma, a familiar pungent smell, wafts out of nowhere, momentarily reminding me that the old people of the King River tribe have just passed by. Old man Ngidil is here in our midst, still. Dampness, water on dried bamboo, stick and kangaroo sinew spears; the strong odour flares my nostrils. My eyes close. They are there, after all this time. I savour the vision; a tightness forms in my throat, and then the high-pitched ringing sound in my ears. As it becomes deafening and demanding,

227

I ask myself the old question: why is this happening? There is no answer, no way to respond. The only way is to listen and to feel. Yella fella Dreaming.

An Aboriginal voice breaks the spell. 'Gidday, old chap. Might be rain in Wyndham this afternoon.'

'Yeah,' I reply, 'might be. Aargh well.'